EGYPTIAN LANGUAGE

Lessons in Egyptian HIEROGLYPHICS

Sir E.A. Wallis Budge

BARNES & NOBLE BOOKS
NEW YORK

To

HENRY EDWARD JULER, ESQUIRE, F.R.C.S.

ETC., ETC., ETC.,

TO WHOSE SKILL AND KINDNESS

MY EYESIGHT OWES SO MUCH

This edition published by Barnes & Noble, Inc.

1993 Barnes & Noble Books

ISBN 1-56619-060-6 *casebound*
ISBN 0-7607-1578-5 *paperback*

Printed and bound in the United States of America

93 99 00 01 02 MC 9 8 7 6 5 4 3
99 00 01 02 03 MP 9 8 7 6 5 4 3 2 1

FG

PREFACE.

This little book is intended to form an easy introduction to the study of the Egyptian hieroglyphic inscriptions, and has been prepared in answer to many requests made both in Egypt and in England. It contains a short account of the decipherment of Egyptian hieroglyphics, and a sketch of the hieroglyphic system of writing and of the general principles which underlie the use of picture signs to express thought. The main facts of Egyptian grammar are given in a series of short chapters, and these are illustrated by numerous brief extracts from hieroglyphic texts ; each extract is printed in hieroglyphic type and is accompanied by a transliteration and translation. Following the example of the early Egyptologists it has been thought better to multiply extracts from texts rather than to heap up a large number of grammatical details without supplying the beginner with the means of examining their application. In the limits of the following pages it would be impossible to treat Egyptian grammar at any length, while the discussion of details would be quite out of place. The chief object has been to make the beginner familiar with the most common signs and words, so that he may, whilst puzzling out the extracts from texts quoted in illustration of grammatical facts, be able to attack the longer connected texts given in my "First Steps in Egyptian" and in my "Egyptian Reading Book".

Included in this book is a lengthy list of hieroglyphic characters with their values both as phonetics and ideograms. Some of the characters have not yet been satisfactorily identified and the correctness of the positions of these is, in consequence, doubtful; but it has been thought best to follow both the classification, even when wrong, and the numbering of the characters which are found in the list of "Hieroglyphen" printed by Herr Adolf Holzhausen of Vienna.

E. A. WALLIS BUDGE.

CONTENTS.

CHAPTER I.

HIEROGLYPHIC WRITING.

The ancient Egyptians expressed their ideas in writing by means of a large number of picture signs which are commonly called **Hieroglyphics.** They began to use them for this purpose more than seven thousand years ago, and they were employed uninterruptedly until about B. C. 100, that is to say, until nearly the end of the rule of the Ptolemies over Egypt. It is hardly probable that the hieroglyphic system of writing was invented in Egypt, and the evidence on this point now accumulating indicates that it was brought there by certain invaders who came from north-east or central Asia; they settled down in the valley of the Nile at some place between Memphis on the north and Thebes on the south, and gradually established their civilization and religion in their new home. Little by little the writing spread to the north and to the south, until at length hieroglyphics were employed, for state purposes at least, from the coast of the Mediterranean to the most southern portion of the Island of Meroë, that is to say, over a tract of country more than 2000 miles long. A remarkable peculiarity of Egyptian hieroglyphics is the slight modification of form which they suffered during a period of thousands of years, a fact due, no doubt, partly to the material upon which the Egyptians inscribed them, and partly to a conservatism begotten of religious convictions. The Babylonian and Chinese picture characters became modified at so early a period that, some thousands of years before Christ, their original forms were lost. This reference to the modified forms of hieroglyphics brings us at once to the mention of the various ways in which they were written in Egypt, *i. e.*, to the three different kinds of Egyptian writing.

The oldest form of writing is the **hieroglyphic**, in which the various objects, animate and inanimate, for which the characters stand are depicted as accurately as possible. The following titles of one Ptaḥ-ḥetep, who lived at the period of the rule of the IVth dynasty will explain this; by the side of each hieroglyphic is its description.

1.[1]  a mouth
2.  a door made of planks of wood fastened together by three cross-pieces
3.  the fore-arm and hand

[1] The brackets shew the letters which, when taken together, form words.

4.  a lion's head and one fore paw stretched out

5.  see No. 3

6.  doorway surmounted by cornice of small serpents

7.  a jackal

8.  a kind of water fowl

9.  an owl

10.  a growing plant

11.  a cake

12.  a reed to which is tied a scribe's writing tablet or palette, having two hollows in it for red and black ink

13.  see No. 9

14.  see No. 1

15.  the breast of a man with the two arms stretched out

16.  see No. 11

17.  a seated man holding a basket upon his head.

In the above examples of picture signs the objects which they represent are tolerably evident, but a large number of hieroglyphics do not so easily lend themselves to identification. Hieroglyphics were cut in stone, wood, and other materials with marvellous accuracy, at depths varying from $^1/_{16}$ of an inch to 1 inch; the details of the objects represented were given either by cutting or by painting in colours. In the earliest times the mason must have found it easier to cut characters into the stone than to sculpture them in relief; but it is probable that the idea of preserving carefully what had been inscribed also entered his mind, for frequently when the surface outline of a character has been destroyed sufficient traces remain in the incuse portion of it for purposes of identification. Speaking generally, celestial objects are coloured blue, as also are metal vessels and instruments; animals, birds, and reptiles are painted as far as possible to represent their natural colours; the Egyptian man is painted red, and the woman yellow or a pinky-brown colour; and so on. But though in some cases the artist endeavoured to make each picture sign an exact representation of the original object in respect of shape or form and colour, with the result that the simplest inscription became a splendid piece of ornamentation in which the most vivid colours blended harmoniously, in the majority of painted texts which have been preserved to us the artists have not been consistent in the colouring of their signs. Frequently the same tints of a colour are not used for the same picture, an entirely different colour being often employed; and it is hard not to think that the artist or scribe, having come to the end of the paint which should have been employed for one class of hieroglyphics, frequently made use of that which should have been reserved for another. It has been said that many of the objects which are represented by picture signs may be identified by means of the colours with which they are painted, and this is, no doubt, partly true; but the inconsistency of the Egyptian artist often does away entirely with the value of the colour as a means of identification.

Picture signs or hieroglyphics were employed for religious and state purposes from the earliest to the latest times, and it is astonishing to contemplate the labour which must have been expended by the mason in cutting an inscription of any great length, if every character was well and truly made. Side by side with cutters in stone carvers in wood must have existed, and for a proof of the skill which the latter class of handicraftsmen possessed at a time which must be well nigh pre-dynastic, the reader is referred to the beautiful panels in the Gizeh Museum which have been published by Mariette.[1] The hieroglyphics and figures of the deceased are in relief, and are most delicately and beautifully executed;

[1] See *Les Mastaba de l'Ancien Empire.* Paris, 1882, p. 74 ff.

but the unusual grouping of the characters proves that they belong to a period when as yet dividing lines for facilitating the reading of the texts had not been introduced. These panels cannot belong to a period later than the IIIrd, and they are probably earlier than the Ist dynasty. Inscriptions in stone and wood were cut with copper or bronze and iron chisels. But the Egyptians must have had need to employ their hieroglyphics for other purposes than inscriptions which were intended to remain in one place, and the official documents of state, not to mention the correspondence of the people, cannot have been written upon stone or wood. At a very early date the papyrus plant[1] was made into a sort of paper upon which were written drafts of texts which the mason had to cut in stone, official documents, letters, etc. The stalk of this plant, which grew to the height of twelve or fifteen feet, was triangular, and was about six inches in diameter in its thickest part. The outer rind was removed from it, and the stalk was divided into layers with a flat needle; these layers were laid upon a board, side by side, and upon these another series of layers was laid in a horizontal direction, and a thin solution of gum was then run between them, after which both series of layers were pressed and dried. The number of such sheets joined together depended upon the length of the roll required. The papyrus rolls which have come

[1] *Byblus hieraticus*, or *Cyperus papyrus*.

down to us vary greatly in length and width; the finest Theban papyri are about seventeen inches wide, and the longest roll yet discovered is the great Papyrus of Rameses III,[1] which measures one hundred and thirty-five feet in length. On such rolls of papyrus the Egyptians wrote with a reed, about ten inches long and one eighth of an inch in diameter, the end of which was bruised to make the fibres flexible, and not cut; the ink was made of vegetable substances, or of coloured earths mixed with gum and water.

Now it is evident that the hieroglyphics traced in outline upon papyrus with a comparatively blunt reed can never have had the clearness and sharp outlines of those cut with metal chisels in a hard substance; it is also evident that the increased speed at which government orders and letters would have to be written would cause the scribe, unconsciously at first, to abbreviate and modify the picture signs, until at length only the most salient characteristics of each remained. And this is exactly what happened. Little by little the hieroglyphics lost much of their pictorial character, and degenerated into a series of signs which went to form the cursive writing called **Hieratic**. It was used extensively by the priests in copying literary works in all periods, and though it occupied originally a subordinate position in respect of hieroglyphics, especially as regards religious texts, it at length became equal in

[1] Harris Papyrus, No. 1. British Museum, No. 9999.

importance to hieroglyphic writing. The following example of hieratic writing is taken from the Prisse Papyrus upon which at a period about B. C. 2600 two texts, containing moral precepts which were composed about one thousand years earlier, were written.

Now if we transcribe these into hieroglyphics we obtain the following:—

1. a reed
2. a mouth
3. a hare
4. the wavy surface of water
5. see No. 4
6. a kind of vessel
7. an owl
8. a bolt of a door
9. a seated figure of a man
10. a stroke written to make the word symmetrical
11. see No. 1
12. a knee bone (?)
13. see No. 2.
14. a roll of papyrus tied up
15. an eye
16. see No. 6
17. a goose
18. see No. 9
19. see No. 4
20. a chair back
21. a sickle

22.  an eagle

23.  see No. 7

24.  a tree

25.  see No. 14

26.  an axe

27.  see No. 10.

On comparing the above hieroglyphics with their hieratic equivalents it will be seen that only long practice would enable the reader to identify quickly the abbreviated characters which he had before him; the above specimen of hieratic is, however, well written and is relatively easy to read. In the later times, *i. e.*, about B. C. 900, the scribes invented a series of purely arbitrary or conventional modifications of the hieratic characters and so a new style of writing, called **Enchorial** or **Demotic**, came into use; it was used chiefly for business or social purposes at first, but at length copies of the "Book of the Dead" and lengthy literary compositions were written in it. In the Ptolemaic period Demotic was considered to be of such importance that whenever the text of a royal decree was inscribed upon a stele which was to be set up in some public place and was intended to be read by the public in general, a version of the said decree, written in the Demotic character, was added. Famous examples of stelae inscribed in hieroglyphic, demotic, and Greek, are the Canopus Stone, set up at Canopus in the reign of Ptolemy III. Euergetes I. in the ninth year of his reign (B. C. 247—222), and the Rosetta

Stone set up at Rosetta, in the eighth year of the reign of Ptolemy V. Epiphanes (B. C. 205—182).

In all works on ancient Egyptian grammar the reader will find frequent reference to *Coptic.* The Coptic language is a dialect of Egyptian of which four or five varieties are known; its name is derived from the name of the old Egyptian city Qebt, through the Arabic *Qubṭ,* which in its turn was intended to represent the Gr. Αἰγύπτος. The dialect dates from the second century of our era, and the literature written in it is chiefly Christian. Curiously enough Coptic is written with the letters of the Greek alphabet, to which were added six characters, derived from the Demotic forms of ancient Egyptian hieroglyphics, to express sounds which were peculiar to the Egyptian language.

Hieroglyphic characters may be written in columns or in horizontal lines, which are sometimes to be read from left to right and sometimes from right to left. There was no fixed rule about the direction in which the characters should be written, and as we find that in inscriptions which are cut on the sides of a door they usually face inwards, *i. e.,* towards the door, each group thus facing the other, the scribe and sculptor needed only to follow their own ideas in the arrangement and direction of the characters, or the dictates of symmetry. To ascertain the direction in which an inscription is to be read we must observe in which way the men, and birds, and animals face, and then read *towards* them. The two following examples will illustrate this :—

1.

2.

Now on looking at these passages we notice that the men, the chicken, the owls, the hawk, and the hares all face to the left; to read these we must read from left to right, *i. e., towards* them. The second extract has been set up by the compositor with the characters facing in the opposite direction, so that to read these now we must read from right to left (No. 3).

3. 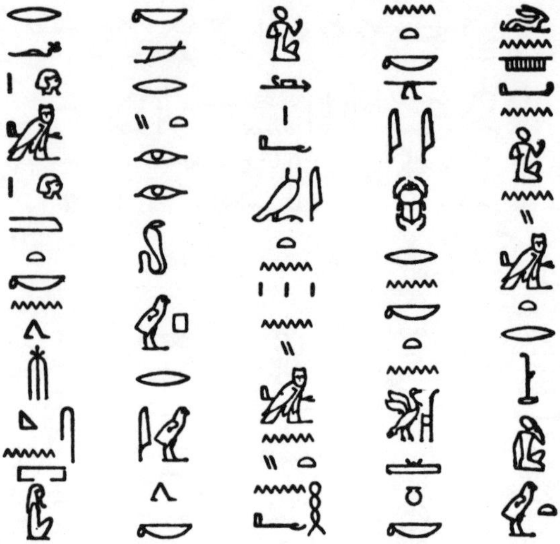

Hieratic is usually written in horizontal lines which are to be read from right to left, but in some papyri dating from the XIIth dynasty the texts are arranged in short columns.

Before we pass to the consideration of the Egyptian Alphabet, syllabic signs, etc., it will be necessary to set forth briefly the means by which the power to read these was recovered, and to sketch the history of the decipherment of Egyptian hieroglyphics in connection with the **Rosetta Stone**.

CHAPTER II

THE ROSETTA STONE AND THE DECIPHERMENT OF HIEROGLYPHICS.

The Rosetta Stone was found by a French artillery officer called Boussard, among the ruins of Fort Saint Julien, near the Rosetta mouth of the Nile, in 1799, but it subsequently came into the possession of the British Government at the capitulation of Alexandria. It now stands at the southern end of the great Egyptian Gallery in the British Museum. The top and right hand bottom corner of this remarkable object have been broken off, and at the present the texts inscribed upon it consist of fourteen lines of hieroglyphics, thirty-two lines of demotic, and fifty-four lines of Greek. It measures about 3 ft. 9 in. × 2 ft. $4^1/_2$ in. × 11 in. on the inscribed side.

The Rosetta Stone records that Ptolemy V. Epiphanes, king of Egypt from B. C. 205 to B. C. 182, conferred great benefits upon the priesthood, and set aside large revenues for the maintenance of the temples, and remitted the taxes due from the people at a period of distress, and undertook and carried out certain costly engineering works in connection with the irrigation system of Egypt. In gratitude for these acts the priesthood convened a meeting at Memphis, and ordered that a statue of the king should be set up in every temple of Egypt, that a gilded wooden statue of the king placed in a gilded wooden shrine should be established in each temple, etc.; and as a part of the great plan to do honour to the king it was ordered that a copy of the decree, inscribed on a basalt stele in hieroglyphic, demotic, and Greek characters, should be set up in each of the first, second, and third grade temples near the king's statue. The provisions of this decree were carried out in the eighth year of the king's reign, and the Rosetta Stone is one of the stelae which, presumably, were set up in the great temples throughout the length and breadth of the land. But the importance of the stone historically is very much less than its value philologically, for the decipherment of the Egyptian hieroglyphics is centred in it, and it formed the base of the work done by scholars in the past century which has resulted in the restoration of the ancient Egyptian language and literature.

It will be remembered that long before the close of the Roman rule in Egypt the hieroglyphic system of writing had fallen into disuse, and that its place had been taken by demotic, and by Coptic, that is to say, the Egyptian language written in Greek letters; the widespread use of Greek and Latin among the governing and upper classes of Egypt also caused the disappearance of Egyptian as the language of state. The study of hieroglyphics was prosecuted by the priests in remote districts probably until the end of the Vth century of our era, but very little later the ancient inscriptions had become absolutely a dead letter, and until the beginning of the last century there was neither an Oriental nor a European who could either read or understand a hieroglyphic inscription. Many writers pretended to have found the key to the hieroglyphics, and many more professed, with a shameless impudence which it is hard to understand in these days, to translate the contents of the texts into a modern tongue. Foremost among such pretenders must be mentioned Athanasius Kircher who, in the XVIIth century, declared that he had found the key to the hieroglyphic inscriptions ; the translations which he prints in his *Oedipus Aegyptiacus* are utter nonsense, but as they were put forth in a learned tongue many people at the time believed they were correct. More than half a century later the Comte de Pahlin stated that an inscription at Denderah was only a translation of Psalm C., and some later writers believed that the Egyptian inscriptions contained Bible phrases and Hebrew compositions.[1] In the first half of the XVIIIth century Warburton appears to have divined the existence of alphabetic characters in Egyptian, and had he pos-

[1] See my *Mummy*, p. 126.

sessed the necessary linguistic training it is quite possible that he would have done some useful work in decipherment. Among those who worked on the right lines must be mentioned de Guignes, who proved the existence of groups of characters having determinatives, and Zoëga, who came to the conclusion that the hieroglyphics were letters, and what was very important, that the cartouches, *i. e.*, the ovals which occur in the inscriptions and are so called because they resemble cartridges, contained royal names.[1] In 1802 Akerblad, in a letter to Silvestre de Sacy, discussed the demotic inscription on the Rosetta Stone, and published an alphabet of the characters. But Akerblad never received the credit which was his due for this work, for although it will be found, on comparing Young's "Supposed Enchorial Alphabet" printed in 1818 with that of Akerblad printed in 1802, that *fourteen* of the characters are identical in both alphabets, no credit is given to him by Young. Further, if Champollion's alphabet, published in his *Lettre à M. Dacier*, Paris, 1822, be compared with that of Akerblad, sixteen of the characters will be found to be identical; yet Champollion, like Young, seemed to be oblivious of the fact.

With the work of Young and Champollion we reach firm ground. A great deal has been written about the merits of Young as a decipherer of the Egyptian hiero-

[1] *De Usu et Origine Obeliscorum*, Rome, 1797, p. 465.

glyphics, and he has been both over-praised and over-blamed. He was undoubtedly a very clever man and a great linguist, even though he lacked the special training in Coptic which his great rival Champollion possessed. In spite of this, however, he identified correctly the names of six gods, and those of Ptolemy and Berenice; he also made out the true meanings of several ideographs, the true values of six letters[1] of the alphabet, and the correct consonantal values of three[2] more. This he did some years before Champollion published his Egyptian alphabet, and as priority of publication (as the late Sir Henry Rawlinson found it necessary to say with reference to his own work on cuneiform decipherment) must be accepted as indicating priority of discovery, credit should be given to Young for at least this contribution towards the decipherment. No one who has taken the pains to read the literature on the subject will attempt to claim for Young that the value of his work was equal to that of Champollion, for the system of the latter scholar was eminently scientific, and his knowledge of Coptic was wonderful, considering the period when he lived. Besides this the quality of his hieroglyphic work was so good, and the amount of it which he did so great, that in those respects the two rivals ought not to be compared. He certainly knew of Young's results, and the admission by him

[1] *I. e.*,  *i*,  *m*, *n*, *p*, *f*, *t*.

[2] *I. e.*, , , .

that they existed would have satisfied Young's friends, and in no way diminished his own merit and glory.

In the year 1815 Mr. J. W. Bankes discovered on the Island of Philae a red granite obelisk and pedestal which were afterwards removed at his expense by G. Belzoni and set up at Kingston Hall in Dorsetshire. The obelisk is inscribed with one column of hieroglyphics on each side, and the pedestal with twenty-four lines of Greek. In 1822 Champollion published an account of this monument in the *Revue encyclopédique* for March, and discussed the hieroglyphic and Greek inscriptions upon it. The Greek inscription had reference to a petition of the priests of Philae made to Ptolemy, and his wife Kleopatra, and his sister also called Kleopatra, and these names of course occur in it. Champollion argued that if the hieroglyphic inscription has the same meaning as the Greek, these names must also occur in it. Now the only name found on the Rosetta Stone is that of Ptolemy which is, of course, contained in a cartouche, and when Champollion examined the hieroglyphic inscription on the Philae obelisk, he not only found the royal names there, enclosed in cartouches, but also that one of them was identical with that which he knew from the Greek of the Rosetta Stone to be that of Ptolemy. He was certain that this name was that of Ptolemy, because in the Demotic inscription on the Rosetta Stone the group of characters which formed the name occurred over and over again, and in the places where, according to the Greek, they ought to occur. But on the Philae Obelisk the name Kleopatra is mentioned, and in both of the names of Ptolemy and Kleopatra the same letters occur, that is to say L and P; if we can identify the letter P we shall not only have gained a letter, but be able to say at which end of the cartouches the names begin. Now writing down the names of Ptolemy and Kleopatra as they usually occur in hieroglyphics we have :—

Ptolemy 

Kleopatra 

Let us however break the names up a little more and arrange the letters under numbers thus :—

Ptolemy.

1. 2. 3. 4. 5. 6. 7.

Kleopatra.

1. 2. 3. 4. 5. 6. 7. 8. 9. 10. 11.

We must remember too that the Greek form of the name Ptolemy is Ptolemaios. Now on looking at the two names thus written we see at a glance that letter No. 5 in one name and No. 1 in the other are identical, and judging by their position only in the names they must represent the letter P; we see too that letter No. 2

in one name and No. 4 in the other are also identical, and arguing as before from their position they must represent the letter L. We may now write down the names thus :—

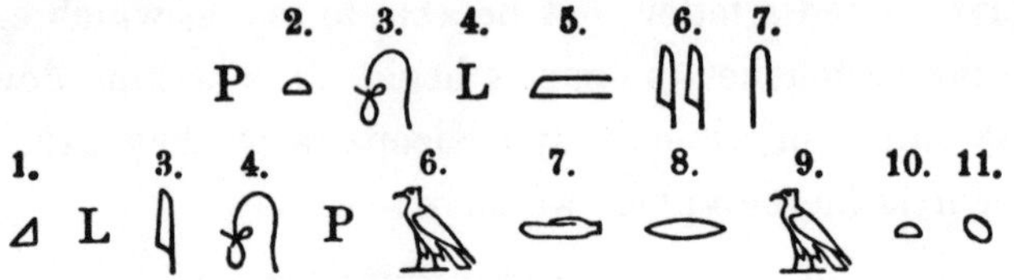

As only one of the names begin with P, that which begins with that letter must be Ptolemy. Now letter No. 4 in one name, and letter No. 3 in the other are identical, and also judging by their position we may assign it in each name the value of some vowel sound like O, and thus get :—

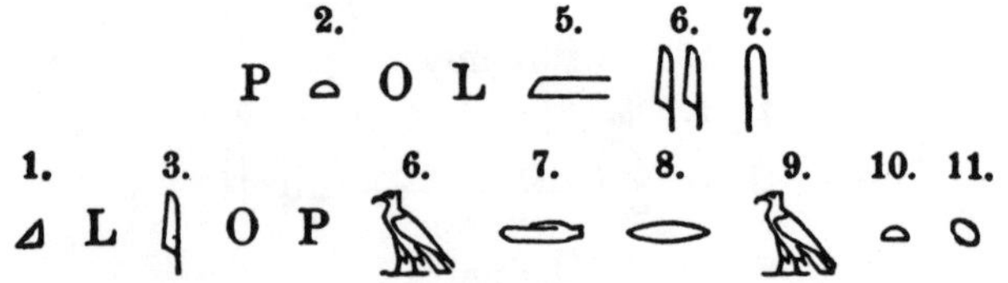

But the letter between P and O in Ptolemy must be T, and as the name ends in Greek with S, the last letter in hieroglyphics must be S, so we may now write down the names thus :—

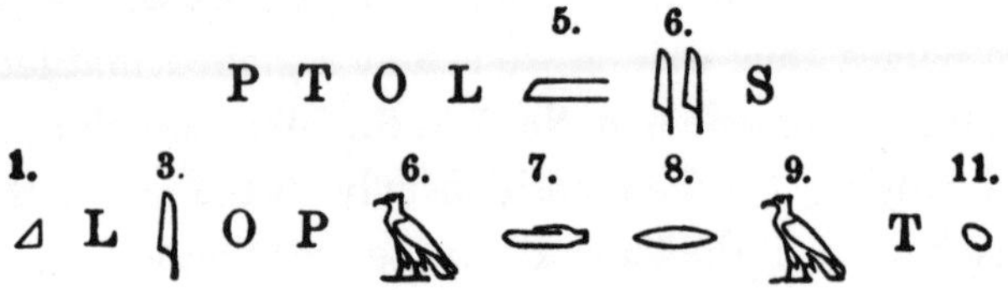

Now if we look, as Champollion did, at the other ways in which the name of Kleopatra is written we shall find that instead of the letter  we sometimes have the letter  which we already know to be T, and as in the Greek form of the name this letter has an A before it, we may assume that  = A; the initial letter must, of course, be K. We may now write the names thus :—

5. 6.

P T O L   S

3. 8. 11.

K L  O P A T  A T 

The sign  (No. 3) in the name Kleopatra represents some vowel sound like E, and this sign doubled (No. 6) represents the vowels AI in the name Ptolemaios; but as  represent EE, or Î, that is to say I pronounced in the Continental fashion, the O of the Greek form has no equivalent in hieroglyphics. That leaves us only the signs ,  and  to find values for. Young had proved that the signs  always occurred at the ends of the names of goddesses, and that  was a feminine termination; as the Greek kings and queens of Egypt were honoured as deities, this termination was added to the names of royal ladies also. This disposes of the signs , and the letters  (No. 5) and  (No. 8) can be nothing else but M and R. So we may now write :—

P T O L M I S, *i. e.*, Ptolemy,

K L E O P A T R A, *i. e.*, Kleopatra.

Now a common title of the Roman Emperors was written hieroglyphically

1. 2. 3. 4. 5.

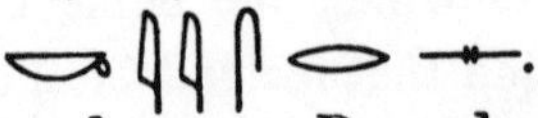

We know that = I, = S, and = R; and as is used as a variant for the first sign in the name of Kleopatra given above, must be K also. The last sign is interchanged with , and we may thus write under the hieroglyphics the values as follows:—

K I S R S

that is to say Καισαρος or Caesar. From the different ways in which the name of Ptolemy is written we learn that = U, and that has also the same value, and that has the same value as , *i. e.*, M, is also apparent. Now we may consider a common Greek name which is written in hieroglyphics ; we may break it up thus:—

1. 2. 3. 4. 5. 6. 7. 8. 9.

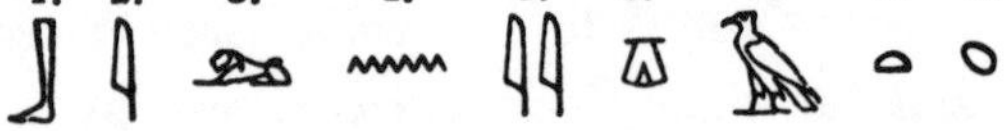

Of these characters we have already identified Nos. 2, 3, 5, 7, 8 and 9, and from the two last we know that we are dealing with the name of a royal lady. But there is also another common Greek name which may be written out in this form:—

1. 2. 3. 4. 5. 6. 7. 8.

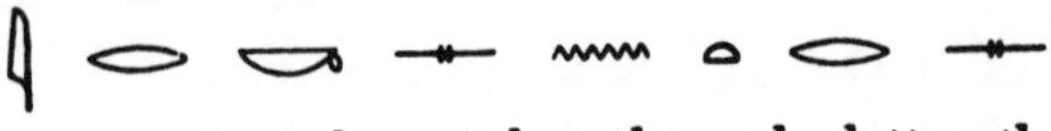

and we see at a glance that the only letter that we

have not met with before is 𓈖. Reading the values of this last group of signs we get E R (*or* L) K S T R (*or* L) S, which can be nothing else but Eleks-ntrs or "Alexander"; thus we find that 𓈖 = N. Now substituting this value for sign No. 4 in the royal lady's name given above we read . E R N I . A T ; and as the Greek text of the inscription in which this name occurs mentions Berenike, we conclude at once that No. 1 sign 𓃀 = B, and that No. 6 sign 𓎡 = K. From other Greek and Latin titles and names we may obtain the values of many other letters and syllables, as will be seen from the following :—

1.  P.H.I.U.L.I.U.P.U (*or* UA).S., *i. e.*, Philip.

2.  P.I.L.A.T.R.A., *i. e.*, Philotera.

3.  BA.R.N.I.K.T., *i. e.*, Berenice.

4.  A.R.R.S.N.A.T., *i. e.*, Arsinoë.

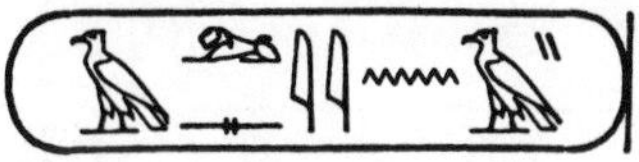 A.R.S.I.N.A.I., *i. e.*, Arsinoë.

5.  T.R.A.P.N.T., *i. e.*, Tryphaena.

6.  T.BA.R.I.S.K.I.S.R.S., *i. e.*, Tiberius Caesar.

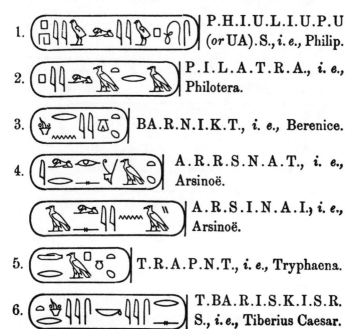

7. 

K-A-I-S K-A-I-S-R-S K-R-M-

i. e., Gaius Caesar Germ-

NI-K-I-S

anicus.

8. 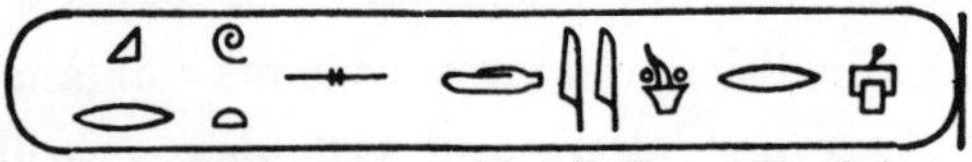

K-L-UT-S T-I-BA-R-SA

i. e., Claudius Tiberius.

9. 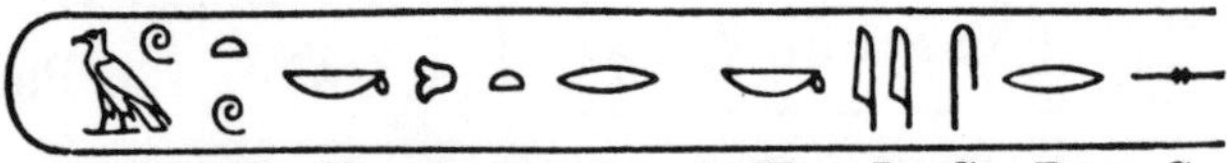

A-U-TU-K-R-T-R K-I-S-R-S

i. e., Autocrator Caesar.

T-A-T-A-S A-R-I-S A-T-R-I-N-S

Titus Aelius Hadrianus.

10. 

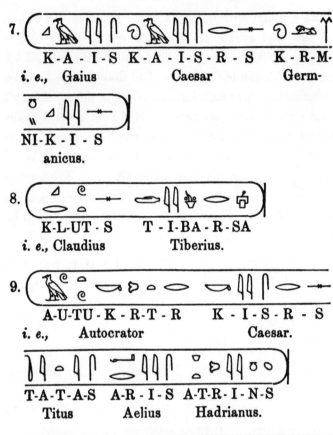

A-U-R-L A-I-S AN-TA-N-I-N-S

i. e., Aurelius Antoninus.

In the Ptolemaic and Roman times the titles of the kings or emperors were often included in the cartouches, and from some of these Champollion derived a number of letters for his Egyptian alphabet. Thus many kings call themselves 𓊪𓏏𓎛 𓌻, and 𓋹 𓆓𓏏𓇾, which appellations were known to mean "Of Ptah beloved" and "living ever". Now in the first of these 𓊪𓏏𓎛 𓌻 we know, from the names which we have read above, that the first two signs are P and T, *i. e.*, the first two letters of the name Ptah; the third sign 𓎛 must then have the value of H or of some sound like it. If these three signs 𓊪𓏏𓎛 form the name of Ptah, then the fourth sign 𓌻 must mean "beloved". Now as Coptic is only a dialect of Egyptian written in Greek letters we may obtain some help from it as Champollion did; and as we find in that dialect that the ordinary words for "to love" are *mei* and *mere*, we may apply one or other of these values to the sign 𓌻. In the same way, by comparing variant texts, it was found that 𓋹 was what is called an ideograph meaning "life", or "to live"; now the Coptic word for "life" or "to live", is *ônkh*, so the pronunciation of the hieroglyphic sign must be something like it. We find also that the variant spellings of 𓋹 give us 𓋹𓈖𓐍, and as we already know that 𓈖 = N, the third sign 𓐍 must be KH; incidentally, too, we discover that 𓋹 has the syllabic value of *ānkh*, and that the *ā* has become *ô* in Coptic. If, in the appellation 𓋹 𓆓𓏏𓇾, *i. e.*, "living ever", 𓋹 means "life", it is clear that 𓆓𓏏𓇾 must mean "ever". Of the three signs which form the word we already know the last two, 𓏏 and 𓇾, for we have seen the first in the name Ptolemy, and the second in the name Antoninus, where they have the values of T and TA respectively. Now it was found by comparing certain words written in hieroglyphics with their equivalents in Coptic that the third sign  was the equivalent of a letter in the Coptic alphabet which we may transliterate by TCH, *i. e.*, the sound which *c* has before *i* in Italian. Further investigations carried on in the same way enabled Champollion and his followers to deduce the syllabic values of the other signs, and at length to compile a classified syllabary. We may now collect the letters which we have gathered together from the titles and names of the Greek and Roman rulers of Egypt in a tabular form thus :—

It will be noticed that we have three different kinds of the K sound, three of the T sound, two of the H sound, and three A sounds. At the early date when the values of the hieroglyphics were first recovered it was not possible to decide the exact difference between the varieties of sounds which these letters represented; but the reader will see from the alphabet on pp. 31, 32 the values which are generally assigned to them at the present time. It will be noticed, too, that among the letters of the Egyptian alphabet given above there are no equivalents for F and SH, but these will be found in the complete alphabet.

CHAPTER III.

HIEROGLYPHICS AS IDEOGRAPHS, PHONETICS, AND DETERMINATIVES.

Every hieroglyphic character is a picture of some object in nature, animate or inanimate, and in texts many of them are used in more than one way. The simplest use of hieroglyphics is, of course, as pictures, which we may see from the following :—  a hare ;  an eagle ;  a duck ;  a beetle ;  a field with plants growing in it ; ★ a star ;  a twisted rope ; a comb ;  a pyramid, and so on. But hieroglyphics may also represent *ideas, e. g.*,  a wall falling down sideways represents the idea of "falling" ;  a hall in which deliberations by wise men were made represents the idea of "counsel" ;  an axe represents the idea of a divine person or a god ;  a musical instrument represents the idea of pleasure, happiness, joy, goodness, and the like. Such are called **ideographs.** Now every picture of every object must have had a name, or we may say that each picture was a word-sign ; a list of all these arranged in proper order would have made a dictionary in the earliest times. But let us suppose that at the period when these pictures were used as pictures only in Egypt, or wherever they first appeared, the king wished to put on record that an embassy from some such and such a neighbouring potentate had visited him with such and such an object, and that the chief of the embassy, who was called by such and such a name, had brought him rich presents from his master. Now the scribes of the period could, no doubt, have reduced to writing an account of the visit, without any very great difficulty, but when they came to recording the name of the distinguished visitor, or that of his master, they would not find this to be an easy matter. To have written down the name they would be obliged to make use of a number of hieroglyphics or picture characters which represented most closely the sound of the name of the envoy, without the least regard to their meaning as pictures, and, for the moment, the picture characters would have represented sounds only. The scribes must have done the same had they been ordered to make a list of the presents which the envoy had brought for their royal master. Passing over the evident anachronism let us call the envoy "Ptolemy", which name we may write, as in the preceding chapter, with the signs :—

1. 2. 3. 4. 5. 6. 7.

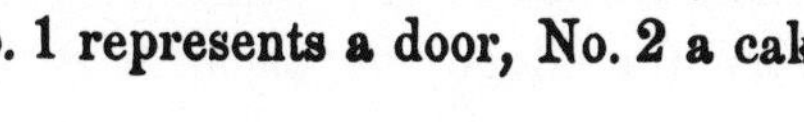

Now No. 1 represents a door, No. 2 a cake, No. 3 a

knotted rope, No. 4 a lion, No. 5 (uncertain), No. 6 two reeds, and No. 7 a chairback; but here each of these characters is employed for the sake of its *sound* only.

The need for characters which could be employed to express *sounds only* caused the Egyptians at a very early date to set aside a considerable number of picture signs for this purpose, and to these the name of **phonetics** has been given. Phonetic signs may be either **syllabic** or **alphabetic,** *e. g.,* *peḥ,* *mut,* *maāt,* *χeper,* which are syllabic, and *p,* *b,* *m,* *r,* *k,* which are alphabetic. Now the five alphabetic signs just quoted represent as pictures, a door, a foot and leg, an owl, a mouth, and a vessel respectively, and each of these objects no doubt had a name; but the question naturally arises how they came to represent single letters? It seems that the sound of the *first letter* in the name of an object was given to the picture or character which represented it, and henceforward the character bore that phonetic value. Thus the first character P, represents a door made of a number of planks of wood upon which three cross-pieces are nailed. There is no word in Egyptian for door, at all events in common use, which begins with P, but, as in Hebrew, the word for door must be connected with the root "to open"; now the Egyptian word for "to open" is *pt[a]ḥ,* and as we know that the first character in that word has the sound of P and of no other letter, we may reasonably assume that the Egyptian word for "door" began with P. The third character  M represents the horned owl, the name of which is preserved for us in the Coptic word *mûlotch* (ⲙⲟⲩⲗⲟϫ); the first letter of this word begins with M, and therefore the phonetic value of  is M. In the same way the other letters of the Egyptian alphabet were derived, though it is not always possible to say what the word-value of a character was originally. In many cases it is not easy to find the word-values of an alphabetic sign, even by reference to Coptic, a fact which seems to indicate that the alphabetic characters were developed from word-values so long ago that the word-values themselves have passed out of the written language. Already in the earliest dynastic inscriptions known to us hieroglyphic characters are used as pictures, ideographs and phonetics side by side, which proves that these distinctions must have been invented in pre-dynastic times.

The Egyptian alphabet is as follows:—

	A	(א)		F	(פ)
	Ȧ	(')	 or 	M	(מ)
	Ā	(ע)	 or 	N	(נ)
 or 	I	(י)	 or 	R and L	(ר, ל)
 or 	U	(ו)		H	(ה)
	B	(ב)		Ḥ	(ח)
	P	(פ)		KH	(χ) (Arab. خ)

	S	(ס)		Ḳ	(ג)
	S	(שׂ)		T	(תּ)
	SH (Ś)	(ש)		Ṭ	(ט)
	K	(כ)	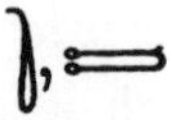	TH (θ)	(ת)
	Q	(ק)		TCH (T')	(צ)

The Egyptian alphabet has a great deal in common with the Hebrew and other Semitic dialects in respect of the guttural and other letters, peculiar to Oriental peoples, and therefore the Hebrew letters have been added to shew what I believe to be the general values of the alphabetic signs. It is hardly necessary to say that differences of opinion exist among scholars as to the method in which hieroglyphic characters should be transcribed into Roman letters, but this is not to be wondered at considering that the scientific study of Egyptian is only about ninety years old, and that the whole of the literature has not yet been published.

Some ideographs have more than one phonetic value, in which case they are called **polyphones**; and many ideographs representing entirely different objects have similar values, in which case they are called homophones.

As long as the Egyptians used picture writing pure and simple their meaning was easily understood, but when they began to spell their words with alphabetic signs and syllabic values of picture signs, which had no reference whatever to the original meaning of the signs, it was at once found necessary to indicate in some way the meaning and even sounds of many of the words so written; this they did by adding to them signs which are called **determinatives.** It is impossible to say when the Egyptians first began to add determinatives to their words, but all known hieroglyphic inscriptions not pre-dynastic contain them, and it seems as if they must have been the product of prehistoric times. They, however, occur less frequently in the texts of the earlier than of the later dynasties.

Determinatives may be divided into two groups; those which determine a single species, and those which determine a whole class. The following determinatives of classes should be carefully noted:—

Character	Determinative of	Character	Determinative of
1. 	to call, beckon	6.  or 	god, divine being or thing
2. 	man	7. 	goddess
3. 	to eat, think, speak, and of whatever is done with the mouth	8. 	tree
		9. 	plant, flower
		10. 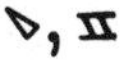	earth, land
4. 	inertness, idleness	11. 	road, to travel
5. 	woman	12. 	foreign land

	Character	Determinative of
13.		nome
14.		water
15.		house
16.		to cut, slay
17.		fire, to cook, burn
18.		smell (good or bad)
19.		to overthrow
20.		strength
21.		to walk, stand, and of actions performed with the legs
22.		flesh
23.		animal
24.		bird
25.		little, evil, bad
26.		fish
27.		rain, storm
28.		day, time
29.		village, town, city
30.		stone
31.	 or 	metal
32.		grain
33.		wood
34.		wind, air
35.		foreigner
36.		liquid, unguent
37.		abstract
38.		crowd, collection of people
39.		children.

A few words have no determinative, and need none, because their meaning was fixed at a very early period, and it was thought unnecessary to add any ; examples of such are *ḥenā*[1] "with", *ȧm* "in", *māk* "verily" and the like. On the other hand a large number of words have one determinative, and several have more than one. Of words of one determinative the following are examples :—

1. *ȧm* to eat; a picture of a man putting food into his mouth is the determinative.
2. *ānχ* a flower; the picture of a flower is the determinative.
3. *sma* to slay; the picture of a knife is the determinative, and indicates that the word *sma* means "knife", or that it refers to some action that is done with a knife.
4. *ses* bolt; the picture of the branch of a tree is the determinative, and indicates that *ses* is an object made of wood.

Of words of one or more determinatives the following are examples :—

1. *renpit* flowers; the pictures of a flower in the bud, and a flower, are the determinatives; the three strokes ꞁꞁꞁ are the sign of the plural.

[1] Strictly speaking there is no *e* in Egyptian, and it is added in the transliterations of hieroglyphic words in this book simply to enable the reader to pronounce them more easily.

2. 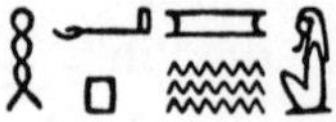 *Ḥāp* god of the Nile ; the pictures of water enclosed by banks , and running water , and a god are the determinatives.

3.  *nemmeḥu* poor folk ; the pictures of a child , and a man , and a woman are the determinatives, and shew that the word *nemmeḥ* means a number of human beings, of both sexes, who are in the condition of helpless children.

Words may be spelt (1) with alphabetic characters wholly, or (2) with a mixture of alphabetic and syllabic characters ; examples of the first class are :—

	*sfenṭ*	a knife
	*àsfet*	wickedness
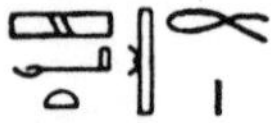	*šāt*	a book
	*uàa*	a boat
	*ḥeqer*	to be hungry, hunger
	*semeḥi*	left hand side
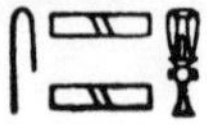	*sešeš*	a sistrum.

And examples of the second class are :—

1. 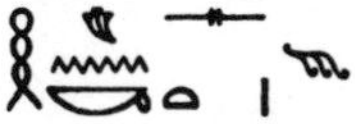 *ḥenkset* hair, in which  has by itself the value of *ḥen*; so the word might be written 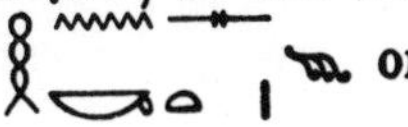 or 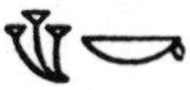 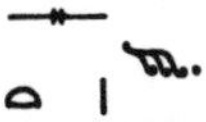.

2.  *neḥebet* neck, in which  has by itself the value of *neḥ*; so the word might be written  as well as .

3. 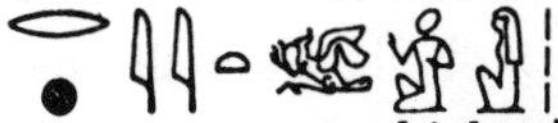 *reχit* men and women, in which  has by itself the value of *reχit*; thus in  the word is actually written twice, for 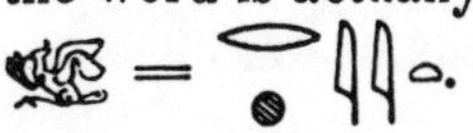.

In many words the last letter of the value of a syllabic sign is often written in order to guide the reader as to its pronunciation. Take the word . The ordinary value of  is *mesfer* "car", but the  which follows it shews that the sign is in this word to be read *mesfem*, and the determinative indicates that the word means that which is smeared under the eye, or "eye-paint, stibium". For convenience' sake we may call such alphabetic helps to the reading of words **phonetic complements.** The following are additional examples, the phonetic complement being marked by an asterisk.

	mester	ear
	ḥai	rain
	šenār	storm
	merḥu	unguent
	ḥememu	mankind.

We may now take a short extract from the Tale of the Two Brothers, which will illustrate the use of alphabetic and syllabic characters and determinatives; the determinatives are marked by *, and the syllabic characters by †; the remaining signs are alphabetic. (N. B. There is no *e* in Egyptian.)

un *àn* *paif* *sen* *āa* *ḥer*
His brother elder

χeperu *mà* *àbu* *shemātu* *àu-f* *ḥer*
became like panthers southern. He

ṭāt *ṭemtu* *paif* *nui*
made sharp his dagger,

àu-f ḥer ṭātu-f em ṭet-f un àn

he placed it in his hand.

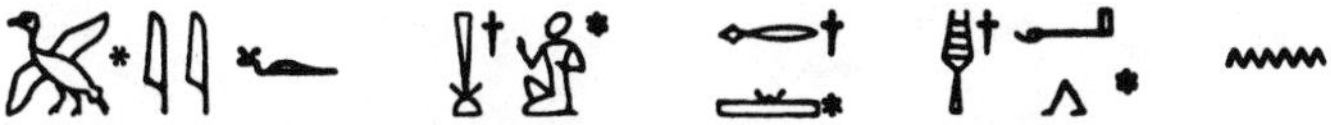

paif sen āa āḥā en

His brother elder stood

ḥa pa sbai paif

behind the door of his

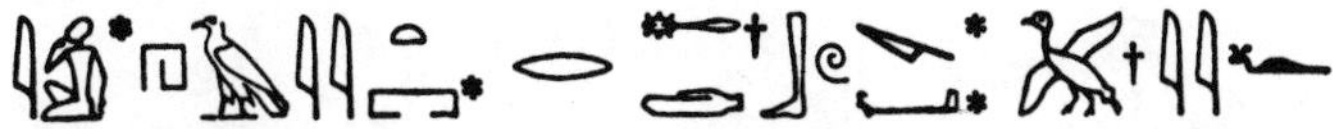

àhait er χaṭbu paif

stable to stab his

sen śeràu em paif i em

brother younger at his coming at

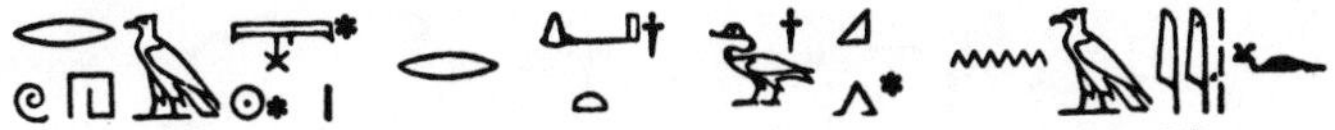

ruha er˙ ṭāt āq naif

eventide to make to enter his

àaut er pa àhait

cattle into the stables.

χer ȧr pa Šu ḥer ḥetep ȧu-f

Now when the god Shu was setting he

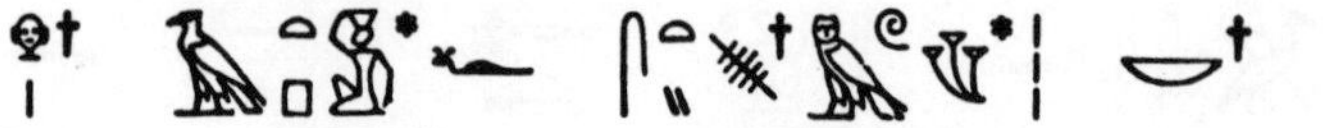

ḥer atep-f stimu neb

was loading himself with green herbs of all kinds

en seχet em paif seχeru

of the fields according to his habit

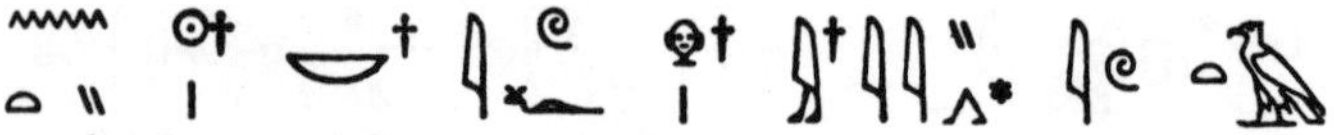

enti hru neb ȧu-f ḥer i ȧu ta

of day every, he was coming [home]. The

ȧḥt ḥāuti ḥer āq er pa

cow leading entered into the

ȧhait ȧu set ḥer teṭ en

stable, she said to

pai-set saȧu mākuȧ paik

her keeper, Verily thy

sen āa āḥā er ḥāt-tuk χeri

brother elder standeth in front of thee with

paif nui er χaṭbu - k

his dagger to stab thee;

ruȧ - k tu er - ḥāt - f un ȧn - f

run away from before him. He

ḥer setem pa ṭeṭ taif ȧḥ

hearkened unto the speech of his cow

ḥāuti ȧu ta ket-θȧ ḥer āq

leading. The next entered, [and]

ȧu set ḥer ṭeṭ - θȧ - f em mȧtet ȧuf

she was saying to him likewise. He

ḥer ennu χeri pa sba en

looked under the door of

paif *àhait* *àuf* *ḥer*

his stable, he

petrà *reṭ* *en* *paif*

saw the legs of his

sen *āa* *àuf* *āḥā* *en* *ḥa*

brother elder [as] he stood behind

pa *sba* *àu* *paif* *nui*

the door his dagger

em *ṭet-f* *àuf* *ḥer* *uaḥ* *taif*

in his hand. He set his

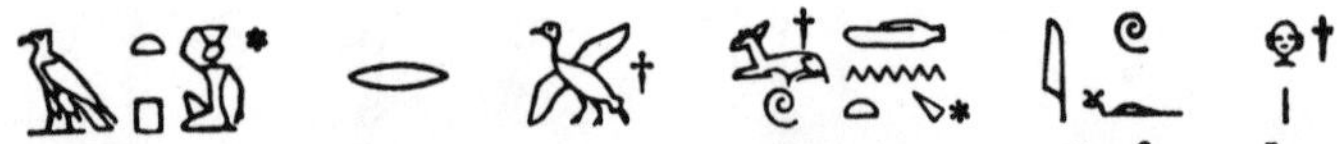

atep *er* *pa* *àuṭent* *àuf* *ḥer*

load upon the ground, he betook

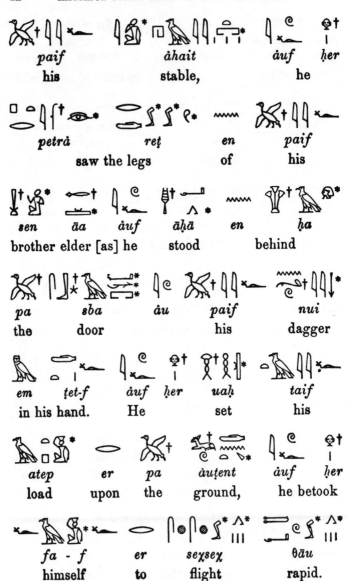

fa - f *er* *seχseχ* *θāu*

himself to flight rapid.

CHAPTER IV.[1]

A SELECTION OF HIEROGLYPHIC CHARACTERS WITH THEIR PHONETIC VALUES, ETC.

1. Figures of Men.

		Phonetic value.	Meaning as ideograph or determinative.
1.		*enen*	man standing with inactive arms and hands, submission
2.		*à*	to call, to invoke
3.		*kes* (?)	man in beseeching attitude, propitiation
5.		*ṭua*	to pray, to praise, to adore, to entreat
6.		*ṭua*	(to pray, to praise, to adore, to entreat)
7.		*hen*	to praise
8.		*qa, ḥāā*	to be high, to rejoice
9.		*ān*	man motioning something to go back, to retreat

[1] The numbers and classification of characters are those given by Herr Adolf Holzhausen in his *Hieroglyphen*.

10.		*ȧn*	man calling after someone, to beckon
11.		*ȧn*	
12.		—	see No. 7
13.		—	see No. 10
14.			man hailing some one
15.		*ȧb*	to dance
16.		*ȧb*	to dance
17.		*ȧb*	to dance
18.		*ȧb*	to dance
19.		*kes*	man bowing, to pay homage
20.		*kes*	man bowing, to pay homage
21.		—	man running and stretching forward to reach something
22.		*sati*	to pour out water, to micturate
23.			
24.		*ḥeter*	two men grasping hands, friendship
25.		*ȧmen*	a man turning his back, to hide, to conceal

26.	*nem*	pygmy
27.	*tut, sāḥu, qeres*	image, figure, statue, mummy, transformed dead body
28.	*tetta*	a dead body in the fold of a serpent
29.	*ur, ser*	great, great man, prince, chief
30.	*àau, ten*	man leaning on a staff, aged
31.	*neχt*	man about to strike with a stick, strength
32.	—	man stripping a branch
33.	*ṭua*	. . . .
34.	*seḥer*	to drive away
35.	*χeχeθ* (?)	two men performing a ceremony (?)
36.	*ṡema* (?)	. . . .
37.	*àḥi*	man holding an instrument
38.	—	man holding an instrument
39.	—	man about to perform a ceremony with two instruments
40.	*neχt*	see No. 31
41.	—	to play a harp

42.		—	to plough
43.		*ṭā*	to give a loaf of bread, to give
44.		*sa*	to make an offering
45.		*nini*	man performing an act of worship
46.		*āb*	man throwing water over himself, a priest
47.		*sati, set*	man sprinkling water, purity
48.		—	a man skipping with a rope
49.		*χus*	man building a wall, to build
50.		—	man using a borer, to drill
51.		*qeṭ*	to build
52.		*fa, kat*	a man with a load on his head, to bear, to carry, work
53.		*āχ*	man supporting the whole sky, to stretch out
54.		*fa*	to bear, to carry; see No. 52
55.		*χesṭeb*	man holding a pig by the tail......
56.		*qes*	to bind together, to force something together
57.		*qes*	
58.		*ḥeq*	man holding the *ḥeq* sceptre, prince, king

59.		—	prince, king
62.		—	prince or king wearing White crown
63.		—	prince or king wearing Red crown
65.		—	prince or king wearing White and Red crowns
68.		*ur*	great man, prince
69.		*ur*	
70.		*àθi*	prince, king
71.		*ḥen*	a baby sucking its finger, child, young person
72.		*ḥen*	a child
74.		*ḥen*	a child wearing the Red crown
75.		*ḥen*	a child wearing the disk and uraeus
76.		*mesṭem*	. . . .
78.			
79.		*χefti*	a man breaking in his head with an axe or stick, enemy, death, the dead
80.			
82.		*māšā*	man armed with a bow and arrows, bowman, soldier
83.		*menf*	man armed with shield and sword, bowman, soldier

84.		—	man with his hands tied behind him, captive
85.		—	man with his hands tied behind him, captive
86.		—	man tied to a stake, captive
87.		—	man tied by his neck to a stake
88.		—	beheaded man tied by his neck to a stake
89.		*sa, remt*	man kneeling on one knee
90.		*ȧ*	to cry out to, to invoke
91.		*ȧ*	man with his right hand to his mouth, determinative of all that is done with the mouth
92.		*enen*	submission, inactivity
93.		*hen*	to praise
94.		*ṭua*	to pray, to praise, to adore, to entreat
96.		*ȧmen*	to hide
97.		—	to play a harp
98.		*ȧuḥ, sur*	to give or offer a vessel of water to a god or man
99.		*sa*	to make an offering
100.		*ȧmen, ḥab*	man hiding himself, to hide, hidden
101.		*āb*	man washing, clean, pure, priest

102.		*āb*	man washing, clean, pure, priest
103.			
104.			
105.		*fa, kat*	man carrying a load; see No. 52
106.		*ḥeḥ*	man wearing emblem of year, a large, indefinite number
107.		*ḥeḥ*	a god wearing the sun's disk and grasping a palm branch in each hand
108.		—	to write
110.		—	dead person who has obtained power in the next world
111.		—	dead person, holy being
112.		—	dead person, holy being
113.		—	a sacred or divine person
114.		—	a sacred or divine king
115.		—	divine or sacred being holding the sceptre 
116.		—	divine or sacred being holding the sceptre 
117.		—	divine or sacred being holding the whip or flail 
119.		—	divine or sacred being holding  and 

120.		—	king wearing the White crown and holding  and 
121.		—	king wearing the Red crown and holding  and 
123.		—	king wearing the Red and White crowns and holding 
124.		—	king wearing the Red and White crowns and holding 
125.		—	ibis-headed being, Thoth
126.		*sa*	a sacred person holding a cord? a guardian?
127.		*sa*	a sacred person holding a cord? a guardian?
128.		*sa*	a watchman, to guard, to watch
129.		—	a sacred person, living or dead
130.		—	a sacred person, living or dead
131.		*šeps*	a sacred person
132.		*neťem*	a person sitting in state
133.		*χer*	to fall down
134.		*mit*	a dead person
135.		*meḥ*	to swim
136.		*neb*	a man swimming, to swim
137.		*neb*	a man swimming, to swim

2. Figures of Women

No.	Sign	Transliteration	Meaning
1.		*ḥeter*	two women grasping hands, friendship
3.		*θehem*	woman beating a tambourine, to rejoice
4.		*ḳeb*	to bend, to bow
5.		*Nut*	the goddess Nut, *i. e.*, the sky
6.		—	woman with dishevelled hair
7.		*sat* (?)	a woman seated
8.		—	a sacred being, sacred statue
9.		—	
10.		—	a divine or holy female, or statue
11.		—	
12.		*ȧri*	a guardian, watchman
13.		*θehem*	see No. 3
14.		*beq*	a pregnant woman
15.		*mes, pāpā*	a parturient woman, to give birth
16.		*menā*	to nurse, to suckle a child
17.		*renen*	to dandle a child in the arms

8. Figures of Gods and Goddesses.

No.	Sign	Transliteration	Meaning
1.		*Ȧusȧr* (or *Ȧsȧr*)	the god Osiris
3.		*Ptaḥ*	the god Ptaḥ
4.		*Ptaḥ*	Ptaḥ holding a sceptre, and wearing a *menȧt* 
6.		*Ta-tunen*	the god Ta-tunen
7.		*Tanen*	the god Tanen
8.		*Ptaḥ-Tanen*	the god Ptaḥ-Tanen
9.		*Ȧn-ḥeru*	the god An-ḥeru
10.		*Ȧmen*	Ȧmen, or Menu, or Ȧmsu in his ithyphallic form.
11.		*Ȧmen*	Ȧmen wearing plumes and holding 
13.		*Ȧmen*	Ȧmen wearing plumes and holding Maāt
14.		*Ȧmen*	Ȧmen wearing plumes and holding a short, curved sword
15.		*Ȧmen*	Ȧmen holding the *user* sceptre 
16.		*Ȧāḥ*	the Moon-god
17.		*χensu*	the god Khensu
18.		*Śu*	the god Shu

19.		*Śu*	the god Shu
20.		*Rā-usr-Maāt*	god Rā as the mighty one of Maāt
21.		*Rā*	the god Rā wearing the white crown
22.		*Rā*	Rā holding sceptres of the horizons of the east and west
23.		*Rā*	Rā holding the sceptre 
24.		*Rā*	Rā wearing disk and uraeus and holding 
25.		*Rā*	Rā wearing disk and uraeus
26.		*Ḥeru*	Horus (*or* Rā) wearing White and Red crowns
27.		*Rā*	Rā wearing disk and holding symbol of "life"
29.		*Rā*	Rā wearing disk, uraeus and plumes, and holding sceptre
31.		*Set*	the god Set
32.		*Ānpu*	the god Anubis
33.		*Teḥuti*	the god Thoth
36.			
37.		*Xnemu*	the god Khnemu
38.			
39.		*Ḥāpi*	the Nile-god

40.		*Åuset* (or *Åst*)	Isis holding papyrus sceptre
41.		*Åuset* (or *Åst*)	Isis holding symbol of "life"
42.		*Åuset* (or *Åst*)	Isis holding papyrus sceptre
45.		*Nebt-ḥet*	Nephthys holding symbol of "life"
51.		*Nut*	the goddess Nut
52.		*Seśeta*	the goddess Sesheta
53.		*Usr-Maāt*	the goddess Maāt with sceptre of strength
54.		*Maāt*	the goddess Maāt
55.			
58.		*Ānqet*	the goddess Ānqet
62.		*Bast*	the goddess Bast
63.		*Seχet*	the goddess Sekhet
64.		*Un*	the hare-god Un
65.			
66.		*Meḥit*	the goddess Meḥit
67.		*Śeta*	a deity
68.		*Seḥer*	a god who frightens, terrifies, or drives away

69.		*Seḥer*	see No. 68
70.			
71.		*Bes*	the god Bes
73.		*χeperȧ*	the god Khepera
74.			

4. Members of the Body.

1.		*ṭep, ṭaṭa*	the head, the top of anything
3.		*ḥer, ḥrȧ*	the face, upon
5, 6, 7.		*šent, ušer*	the hair, to want, to lack
8.		*šere* (?)	a lock of hair
9.	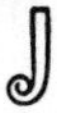	*χabes*	the beard
10.		*mer, maa, ȧri*	the right eye, to see, to look after something, to do
11.		—	the left eye
12.		*maa*	to see
13.		—	an eye with a line of stibium below the lower eye-lid
14.		*rem*	an eye weeping, to cry
15.		*an*	to have a fine appearance

16.		*merti, maa*	the two eyes, to see
17.		*uťat*	the right eye of Rā, the Sun
18.		*uťat*	the left eye of Rā, the Moon
19.		*uťatti*	the two eyes of Rā
20.		*ṭebḥ*	an *utchat* in a vase, offerings
23.		*àr*	the pupil of the eye
24.		*ṭebḥ*	two eyes in a vase, offerings
25.		*àm*	eyebrow
26.		*mesťer*	ear
28.		*χent*	nose, what is in front
29.		*re*	opening, mouth, door
30.		*septi*	the two lips
31.		*sept*	lip raised shewing the teeth
32.		*ārt*	jawbone with teeth
33.		*tef, àṭet*	exudation, moisture
35, 36.		*meṭ*	a weapon or tool
37.		*àat, pesṭ*	the backbone

38.		*śāṭ*	the chine
39.		*menā*	the breast
40, 41.	, 	*seχen*	to embrace
44.			
42.		*ȧn, ȧm*	not having, to be without, negation
47.			
46.		*ka*	the breast and arms of a man, the double
49.		*ser, ṭeser*	hands grasping a sacred staff, something holy
50.			
51.		*χen*	hands grasping a paddle, to transport, to carry away
52.		*āḥa*	arms holding shield and club, to fight
54.		*uṭen*	to write
58.		*χu*	hand holding a whip or flail, to be strong, to reign
59.		*ā, ṭā*	hand and arm outstretched, to give
62.		*meḥ, ermen*	to bear, to carry
63.		*ṭā*	to give
65.		*mā*	to give

66.		*mā, ḥenk*	to offer
67.		—	to offer fruit
68.		*nini*	an act of homage
69.		*neχt*	to be strong, to shew strength
72.		*χerp*	to direct
73, 76.	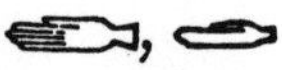	*ṭet*	hand
74.		*šep*	to receive
77.		*kep*	to hold in the hand
82.		*am*	to clasp, to hold tight in the fist
84, 85.		*tebā*	finger, the number 10,000
—		*meter, āq*	to be in the centre, to give evidence
86.		*ān*	thumb
87.		*ān*	thumb
88.		*maā*	a graving tool
90.		*baḥ, met, tai, ka*	phallus, what is masculine, husband, bull
91.		*utet*	to beget
92, 93.	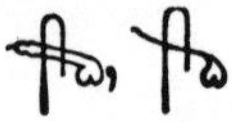	*sem, seshem*	

94		*χerui*	male organs
95.		*ḥem*	woman, female organ
96.		*i*	to go, to walk, to stand
98.		*ān, ḥem*	to go backwards, to retreat
99.		*uār, ret, ment*	to flee, to run away
100.		*teha*	to invade, to attack
101.		*ḳer*	to hold, to possess
102.		*q*	a knee
103.		*b*	a leg and foot
105.		*āb*	arm + hand + leg
106.		*ṭeb*	hand + leg
107.		*āb*	horn + leg
109.		*ḥā*	piece of flesh, limb
111.		*ḥā*	piece of flesh, limb

5. Animals.

1.		*sesem*	horse
2.		*nefer*	horse

3.		*àḥ, ka*	ox
6.		*kaut*	cow
13.		*bà*	calf
14.		*àu*	calt
15.		*ba*	ram
16.		*ba*	Nubian ram of Àmen
17.		*ār*	oryx
19.		*sāḥ*	oryx, the transformed body, the spiritual body
22.		*χen*	a water bag
23.		*āa*	donkey
24.		*uheṛ* (?)	dog
25.		*àmhet*	ape
29.		—	the ape of Thoth
31.		—	ape wearing Red crown
32.		—	ape oearing *utchat* or Eye of the sun
36.		*ma*, or *màau*	lion
38.		*l, r, ru, re*	lion couchant

43.		*χerefu, akeru*	the lions of Yesterday and To-day
44.		*neb*	. . . . . .
47.		*mȧu*	cat
49.		*sab*	jackal, wise person
52.		—	the god Anubis, the god Ȧp-uat
55.		*seśeta*	. . . .
56.		*χeχ*	a mythical animal
57.		—	wild boar
58.		*un*	a hare
59.		*ab*	elephant
61.		*ȧpt*	hippopotamus
62.		*χeb*	rhinoceros
63.		*rer*	pig
65.		*ser*	giraffe
66.		*set*	the god Set, what is bad, death, etc.
68.		*set*	the god Set
69.		*pennu*	rat

5. Members of Animals

3.		*àḥ*	ox
4, 5.	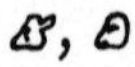	*χent*	nose, what is in front
6.		*χeχ*	head and neck of an ox
8.		*śefit*	strength
9.		—	head and neck of a ram
12.		*śesa*	to be wise
14.		*peḥ*	head and neck of a lion, strength
		*peḥti*	two-fold strength
16.		*ḥā*	head and paw of lion, the fore-part of anything, beginning
21.		*set*	. . . .
22.		*set*	. . . .
24.		*set*	. . . .
30.		*at*	hour, season
33.		*àp*	the top of anything, the forepart
35.		*àat*	rank, dignity
37.		*àpt renpet*	opening of the year, the new year

41.		*āb*	horn, what is in front
44.		*ȧbeḥ*	tooth
45.		*ȧbeḥ*	tooth
46.		*ȧṭen, mester*	to do the duty of someone, vicar, ear, to hear
47.		*peḥ*	to attain to, to end
49.		*χepeš*	thigh
51. 52.		*nem, uḥem*	leg of an animal, to repeat
54.		*kep*	paw of an animal
55, 56.		. . . .	skin of an animal
57. 59.		. . . .	skin of an animal, animal of any kind
60.		*sat*	an arrow transfixing a skin, to hunt
63.		*uā, ȧuā, ȧsu*	bone and flesh, heir, progeny

7. Birds.

1.		*a*	eagle
2.		*maa*	eagle + sickle
3.		*ma*	eagle + 
4.			
6.		*ti, neḫ*	a bird of the eagle class?
7.			
8.		*Ḥeru*	hawk, the god Horus, god
9.		*bak*	hawk with whip or flail
10.		*Ḥerui*	the two Horus gods
11.		*Ḥeru*	Horus with disk and uraeus
12.		*Ḥeru*	Horus wearing the White and Red crowns
13.		*Ḥeru nub*	the "golden Horus"
15.		*neter*	god, divine being, king
16.		*ȧment*	the west
21.		*Ḥeru sma taui*	"Horus the uniter of the two lands"
22.		*Ḥeru Sept*	Horus-Sept

24.		*χu*	. . . .
28.		*āχem, āšem*	sacred form or image
29.		*Ḥeru-šuti*	Horus of the two plumes
30.		*mut, ner*	vulture
33.		*Nebti*	the vulture crown and th uraeus crown
36, 43.	, 	*m*	o̓wl
38.			
39.		*mā*	to give
40.			
41		*mer*	
42.		*embaḥ*	before
45.		*teḥuti*	ibis
46.		*qem*	to find
47.		*ḥam*	to snare, to hunt
48, 51.	, 	*Teḥuti*	the god Thoth
53.		*ba*	the heart-soul
54.		*baiu*	souls

55.		*bak*	to toil, to labour
58.		*χu*	the spirit-soul
60.		*bennu*	a bird identified with the phoenix
61.		*bāḥ*	to flood, to inundate
63.		*uśa*	to make fat
64.		*ṭeśer*	red
65.		*tefa*	bread, cake, food
66.			
67.		*sa*	goose, son
69.		*tefa* (?)	food
70.		*seṭ*	to make to shake with fear, to tremble
71.		*āq*	duck, to go in
72.		*ḥetem*	to destroy
73.		*pa*	to fly
75.		*χen*	to hover, to alight
77.		*qema*, θ*en*	to make, to lift up, to distinguish
78.		*ṭeb*	. . . .

79.		*ur*	swallow, great
80.		*ṡerȧu*	sparrow, little
81.		*ti*	a bird of the eagle kind
82.		*reχit*	intelligent person, mankind
83.		*u*	chicken
87.		*ṭa*	. . . .
88.		*seš*	birds' nest
90.			
91.		*ṡenṭ*	dead bird, fear, terror
92.		*ba*	soul

8. Parts of Birds.

1.		*ṡa, apṭ*	goose, feathered fowl
3.		*ner*	head of vulture
4.		*peḳ*	. . . .
8.		*χu*	head of the *bennu* bird
9.	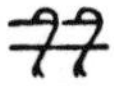	*reχ*	. . . .
10.		*ȧmaχ*	eye of a hawk

11.		*ṭenḥ*	wing, to fly
13.		*śu, maā*	feather, what is right and true
17.		*ermen*	to bear, carry
18.		*śa*	foot of a bird
20.		—	to cut, to engrave
21.		*sa*	son, with ⌓ *t* daughter

9. Amphibious Animals.

1.		*śet*	turtle, evil, bad
2.		*āś*	lizard, abundance
4.		*at, seqa*	crocodile, to gather together
		*ȧθi, ḫenti*	prince
5, 6.	, 	*at*	crocodile
7.		*Sebek*	the god Sebek
8.		*qam*	crocodile skin, black
9.		*Ḥeqt*	the goddess Ḥeqt
10.		*ḥefen*	young frog, 100,000
11.		*āra*	serpent, goddess
16.			

14.		*Meḥent*	the goddess Meḥent
15.			
19.		*åtur*	shrine of a serpent goddess
22.		*ḥef, fenṭ*	worm
24.	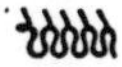	*Āpep*	the adversary of Rā, Apophis
25.		*ṭ, ṭet*	serpent, body
27.		*meṭ*	. . . .
30.		*f*	a cerastes, asp
31.		*sef*	. . . .
32.		*per*	to come forth
33.		*āq*	to enter in
37.		*ptaḥ*	to break open

10. Fish.

1.		*ån*	fish
3.		*betu*	fish
6.		*sepa*	centipede
9.		*nār*	. . . . .

10.		*χa*	dead fish or thing
11.		*bes*	to transport
12.			
14.		*χept*	thigh (?)

11. Insects.

1.		*net, bȧt*	bee
3.		*suten net* (or *bȧt*)	"King of the South and North"
4.		*χeper*	to roll, to become, to come into being
7.		*āf*	fly
8.		*seneḥem*	grasshopper
9.		*serq*	scorpion

12. Trees and Plants.

1, 2.		*ȧm*	tree, what is pleasant
6.		*bener*	palm tree
7.		. . . .	acacia
9.		*χet*	branch of a tree, wood

13, 14.		*renp, ter*	shoot, young twig, year
15, 16, 17.	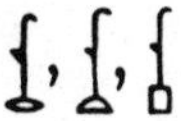		
18.		—	eternal year
19.		—	time
20, 21.		*sept*	a thorn
22.		*neχeb*	shoot, name of a goddess and city
		*enen*	—
24.		*su, suten*	king of the South
25, 27.	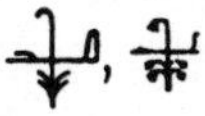	*shemā*	south, name of a class of priestess
26.		*res,*	south
28, 29.		*res*	south
30, 31.			
33.		*à*	feather
		*i*	—
34.		*i*	to go
35.		*seχet*	plants growing in a field
36.		*āb*	an offering

37.		*śa, akh*	lotus and papyrus flowers growing, field
38.			
40.		*ḥen*	cluster of flowers or plants
42, 43.	, 	*ḥa*	cluster of lotus flowers
44.		*meḥt*	the North, the Delta country, the land of the lotus
45.		*res*	the South, the papyrus country
46.			
47.		*uat*	young plant, what is green
48.			
55.		—	flower
58.		*neḥem*	flower bud
62.		—	lotus flower
63.			
67.		*un*	. . . . .
68.		*χa*	flower
70.		*śen*	. . . .
73, 77.	, 	*ut, ut*	to give commands

74, 75.		*ḥet*	white, shining, light
78.		*χesef*	an instrument, to turn back
80.		*mes*	to give birth
81.		—	the union of the South and North
82.		*beti*	barley
83.			
86.		—	grain
88.		*šen*	granary, barn, storehouse
89.			
90.		*ȧrp*	grapes growing, wine
91.			
92.		*mār*	pomegranate
93, 94.		*bener*	sweet, pleasant
96.			
98.		*netem*	sweet, pleasant

13. Heaven, Earth and Water.

1.		*pet, ḥer*	what is above, heaven
2.	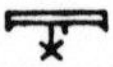	*kerḥ*	sky with a star or lamp, night
3.		*kerḥ*	sky with a star or lamp, night
4.		*àṭet*	water falling from the sky, dew, rain
5.		*θeḥen*	lightning
6.		*qert*	one half of heaven
7.		*Rā, hru*	the Sun-god, day
9.		*χu*	radiance
10, 11.	, 	*Ra*	the Sun-god
13.		*χu, uben*	the sun sending forth rays, splendour
14.		*Sepṭ*	the star Sothis, to be provided with
16.		—	the sun's disk with uraei
17.		—	winged disk
23, 25.	, 	*χā*	the rising sun
26.		*paut*	cake, offering, ennead of gods
28.		*sper*	a rib, to arrive at

29.		*ȧāḥ, ȧbṭ*	moon, month
35.		*sba, ṭua*	star, star of dawn, hour, to pray
36.		*ṭuat*	the underworld
37.		*ta*	land
38.		*ta*	land
40.	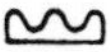	*set* (or *semt*)	mountainous land
41.		—	foreign, barbarian
42.		*ṭu*	mountain, wickedness
44.		*χut*	horizon
45, 46.	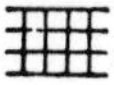, 	*ḥesp, sept*	nome
47.		*ȧṭeb*	the land on one side of the Nile;  = all Egypt
48.		—	land
49.		*uat, ḥer*	a road, a way
50.		*ḳes, m*	side
51, 52.	, 	*ȧner*	stone
53.		*śā* (?)	sand, grain, fruit, nuts
55.		*n*	surface of water, water

		*mu*	water
57.		*mer*	ditch, watercourse, to love
58.			
60.		*sha*	lake
61.	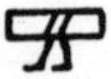	*šem*	to go
62.		—	lake
64.		*Ȧmen*	the god Amen
66.		*ȧa*	island
68.		*χuti*	the two horizons (*i. e.*, East and West)
69.		*peḫ*	swamp, marsh
70.		*ḥemt, bȧa*	metal, iron ore (*or* copper ore?)
71.			
72.			

14. Buildings.

1.		*nu*	town, city
3.		*per*	house, to go out
6.		*per-χeru*	sepulchral meals or offerings

7.		*per ḥet*	"white house", treasury
8.		*h*	quarter of a city (?)
10.		*mer*	
11, 12.	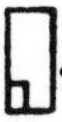, 	*ḥet*	house, temple
13.		*ḥetu*	temples, sanctuaries
14.		*neter ḥet*	god's house
16.		*ḥet āa*	great house
17.		*Nebt-ḥet*	Lady of the house, *i. e.*, Nephthys
19.		*Ḥet-Ḥeru*	House of Horus, *i. e.*, Hathor
29.		*āḥā*	great house, palace
32.		*useχt*	hall, courtyard
36.		*åneb, sebti*	wall, fort
37.		*uhen*	to overthrow
41.		—	fortified town
43.		*seb*	door, gate
44.			
45.		*qenb*	corner, an official

48.	*ḥap*	to hide
51, 52.	—	pyramid
53.	*teχen*	obelisk
54.	*utu*	memorial tablet
55.	*uχa*	pillar
61.	*χaker*	a design or pattern
62.	*seḥ, ārq*	a hall, council-chamber
64.	*seṭ ḥeb* (?)	festival celebrated every thirty years
65.	*ḥeb*	festival
67.		double staircase, to go up
68.	*χet*	staircase, to go up
69.	*āa*	leaf of a door, to open
70.	*s*	a bolt, to close
71.	*ȧs, seb, mes*	to bring, to bring quickly
72, 73.	*θes*	to tie in a knot
74.	*ȧmes*	. . . .
75.	*Ȧmsu*	the god Amsu (or Min ?)
76.	*qeṭ*	. . . .

15. Ships and parts of Ships.

1.		*uȧa, χeṭ*	boat, to sail down stream
2.			
5, 6.	, 	*uḥā*	loaded boat, to transport
14.		—	to sail up stream
16.		*nef, ṭau*	wind, breeze, air, breath
19.		*āḥā*	to stand
21.		*ḥem*	helm, rudder
22.		*χeru*	paddle, voice
23.		*sešep*	. . . .
61.		*ḥennu*	the name of a sacred boat
62.		—	boats of the sun
63.			

16. Seats, Tables, etc.

1.		*ȧst, Ȧuset*	seat, throne, the goddess Isis
2.		*ḥet*	. . . . . .
3.		—	seat, throne

5, 6.	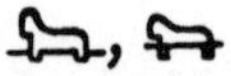	*ȧs*	. . . .
7.		*ster*	to lie down in sleep or death
8.			
9.		*s*	. . . .
11.		*sem, sešem*	. . . .
12.		—	clothes, linen
15.		*serer*	. . . .
16.		*ḥetep*	table of offerings
19.		*χer*	what is under, beneath
20, 22.		---	funeral chest, sarcophagus
23, 24.	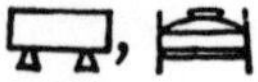		
25.		*ȧat*	zone, district
27.		*ṭeb*	to provide with
28, 29.		*ȧn*	pillar, light tower (?)
30.		*ḥen*	. . . .
31, 33.		*ȧs*	. . . .
36.		*nem*	squeezing juice from grapes, the god Shesmu or Seshmu
37.			

38.		*meter*	to use violence
39.			
41.		*šes*	linen, clothing, garments
43.		*urš*	pillow
44.		*un-ḥrȧ*	mirror
45, 46.*		*serit, χaibit*	fan, shadow
47.		*māχa*	scales, to weigh
50.		*utā*	to balance, to test by weighing
51.			
52, 53, 54.	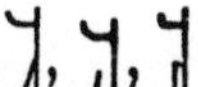	*uθes, res*	to raise up, to wake up
55.			
57.		*maāt*	a reed whistle, what is right or straight
58.		*ȧat*	standard

17. Temple Furniture.

2.		*χaut*	altar
4.		—	fire standard
13.		*neter*	axe or some instrument used in the performance of magical ceremonies

16.		*neter χert*	the underworld
18.		*ṭeṭ*	the tree-trunk that held the dead body of Osiris, stability
20.		*sma*	to unite
22.		*sen*	brother
23.		*śen*	. . . .
26.		*ȧb*	the left side
28.		*ȧm*	to be in
29.		*Seśeta*	name of a goddess

18. Clothing, etc.

1.		*meḥ*	head-gear
7.		*χeperś*	helmet
8.		*ḥet*	the White crown of the South
9.		*res*	the South land
11.		*ṭeśer*	the Red crown of the North
12.		*meḥt*	the North land
13.		*seχeṭ*	the White and Red crowns united
14.		*u, śaā*	cord, one hundred

17.		*śuti*	two feathers
18.		*atef*	plumes, disk and horns
20.			
24.		*meḥ*	crown, tiara
25.		*useχ*	breast plate
26.			
28.		*ȧāḥ*	collar
29.		*sat*	garment of network
30.		*śent*	tunic
32.		*ḥebs*	linen, garments, apparel
34.		*mesen*	
36.		*mer, nes*	tongue, director
38.		*tebt*	sandal
39.		*śen, χetem*	circle, ring
41.		*ṭemt, temṭ*	to collect, to join together
42.		*θet*	buckle
43.		*ānχ*	life

45.		*sefaut*	a seal and cord
46.		*menȧt*	an instrument worn and carried by deities and men
47.		*kep*	. . . . . .
48.		*āper*	to be equipped
50.		*χerp*	to direct, to govern
52.		*seχem*	to be strong, to gain the mastery
56.		*ȧment*	the right side
59.		*χu*	fly-flapper
60.			
61.		*Ȧbt*	the emblem containing the head of Osiris worshipped at Abydos
62.		*ḥeq*	sceptre, to rule
64.		*tchām*	sceptre
65.		*Uast*	Thebes
66.		*usr*	strength, to be strong
73.		*ȧmes*	name of a sceptre
74.		*χu*	flail or whip
76.		*Beb*	the firstborn son of Osiris
77.	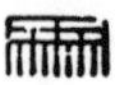	*seχer*	fringe (?)

19. Arms and Armour.

1.		*ăam, neḥes, qema, tebā*	foreign person, to make, finger
		*āq*	what is opposite, middle
3.		*āb*	. . . .
		*seṭeb, seteb*	what is hostile
7, 8.		*qeḥ*	axe
9.		*ṭep*	the first, the beginning
10.		*χepeš*	scimitar
11.		*χaut*	knife
12.		*k*	knife
13.		*qeṭ*	dagger
14, 15.		*ṭes*	knife
19.		*nemmet*	block of slaughter
20.		*sešem*	. . . .
21.		*pet*	bow
25.		*sta,* or *sti*	the front of any thing
26.			

28.		*peṭ*	to stretch out, to extend
33.		*set*	arrow, to shoot
38.		*sa*	the side or back
41.		*āa*	great
42.		*sun*	arrow
43.		*χa*	body
45.		*urit*	chariot
46.			

20. Tools, etc.

1.		*m*	, ...
2.		*tȧt*	emanation
3.		*setep*	to select, to choose
4.		*en*	adze
5.			
7.		*ḥu*	to fight, to smite
8.		*ma*	sickle
9.		*maā*	sickle cutting a reed (?)

12.		*mer, ḥen*	to love
13.		*heb, ār, per*	to plough, hall, growing things
14.		*tem*	to make perfect, the god Temu
15.		*bȧt*	miraculous, wonderful
18.		*sa*	. . . .
19.		*θ*	. . . .
20.		—	metal
21.		*ṭa*	fire-stick (?)
26.		*menχ*	good, to perform
28.		*ḥemt*	workman
29.		*āba*	to open out a way
31.		*ab, (ȧb, āb,) mer*	disease, death
35.		*neṭ*	to break
38.		*uā*	one
40.		*Net*	the goddess Neith
42.		*šes, šems*	to follow after, follower
45.		*qes*	bone

47.		*sek*	estate, farm
48.			
49.		*ḥep*	to hide away
50.		*nub*	gold
53.		*ḥet*	silver
54.		*uasm, smu*	refined copper
55.		*seχet*	fowler's net

21. Cordwork, Network.

1.		*u, śaā*	cord, one hundred
2.		*sta*	to pull, to haul along
5.		*àu*	to be long, extended
		*àmaχ*	pious, sacred
6.		*śes, qes, qeb*	to fetter, linen bandage
8.			
9, 10.	, 	—	to unfasten, book, writing
13.		*ārq*	to bring to the end
15, 16.	, 	*meḥ*	to fill

17.		*śeṭ*	to gain possession of
21.		*āṭ* (*ānt*)	part of a fowler's net
22.			
23.		*šen*	circuit
25.		*senṭ*	outline for foundation of a building
26.		*ua*	magical knot (?)
27.		*ruṭ*	plant, growing things
28.		*sa*	amulet, protection
29.			
30.		*ḥ*	rope
31.		*ḥer*	ḥ + r
32.		*ḥā*	ḥ + ā
34.		*sek*	. . . .
35.			
37.		*uaḥ*	to place, be permanent
39.		*uṭen*	offerings
40.		*ṭeben*	to go round about

41.		*rer, peχer, ṭeben*	to go round about
43.		θ (*th*)	. . . .
44.		θ*et* (?)	to take possession of
45.		*ut*	to bandage, substance which has a strong smell
46.		*set*	flowing liquid

22. Vessels.

1.		*Bast*	name of a city and of a goddess
2.		*Bast*	name of a city and of a goddess
4.		*ḥes*	to sing, to praise, to be favoured
5.		*qebḥ*	cold water, coolness
6.		*ḥen*	king, majesty, servant
7.		*neter ḥen*	divine servant, priest
8.		*χent*	what is in front
9.		*χent*	what is in front
11.		*χnem*	to unite, to be joined to
14.		*ȧrt*	milk
17.		*teχ*	unguent

20.  *ȧrp* wine

21.  *nu, qeṭ, neṭ* liquid

22.  *ȧn* to bring

23.  *ȧb* heart

25. 
26, 27. ,  } *āb, ȧāb* to be clean, ceremonially pure

29.  *mȧ* as, like

31.  *ḥent, āb, useχ* mistress, lady, broad

33.  *ta* cake, bread

37, 38. ,  *χet* fire

39.  *ba* bowl containing grains of incense on fire

40.  *ṭer* bowl containing fruit (?)

41.  *ḳ* libation vase

43.  *neb* lord, all, bowl

44.  *k* flat bowl with ring handle

49. 
50.  } *ḥeb* festival

53., 55.	*ȧt, beti*	grain, barley and the like

23. Offerings.

1, 2., 3, 4., 5, 6.	*ta*	bread, cake
10.	*paut*	bread, cake
	paut	company of nine gods
14.	*sep*	time, season
17.	*χ*	a sieve
22.	*ṭā*	to give
23.	*ter*	. . . .
24.	*χemt*	bronze
	ta	. . . . . .

24. Musical instruments, writing materials, etc.

1.	*ān, sesh*	writing reed, inkpot and palette, to write, to paint
2.	*šāt* (?)	a papyrus roll, book

3.		*mesen*	. . . .
5.		*ḥes*	to play music
6.		*seśeś*	sistrum
8.			
9.		*nefer*	instrument like a lute, good
10.		*Nefer-Temu*	the god Nefer-Temu
11.		*sa*	syrinx, to know
12.		*men*	to abide

25. LINE CHARACTERS, ETC.

1.	I	*uā*	one
2, 4.	III , ¦ —		sign of plural
5.		*ui*	sign of dual
7.	×	*seś*	to split
9.	∩	*met*	ten, ∩∩ = *ṭaut* twenty, ∩∩∩ = *māb* thirty
10.	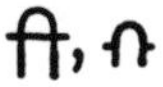	*ḥerit*	fear, awe
11.		*ṭen*	to split, to separate
12.		*t*	cake

14.		*ṭeṭ*	what is said
		*ki ṭeṭ*	"another reading", *i. e.*, variant reading
15.		*qen, set, āṭ*	boundary, border
19.		*ren*	name
20.		*sen*	to depart
22.		*seqer*	captive
25.		*àpt*	part of a palace or temple
27.		*per, àt, beti*	grain, wheat, barley
29, 30.		*nem*	. . . .
38, 40.	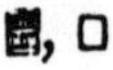	*p*	door
46.		*ḳes*	side, half

CHAPTER V.

PRONOUNS AND PRONOMINAL SUFFIXES.

The personal pronominal suffixes are :—

Sing.	1.	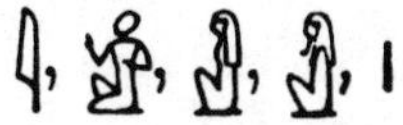	Å
„	2. m.		K
„	2. f.		T, TH (θ)
„	3. m.		F
„	3. f.	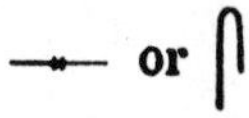	S
Plur.	1.	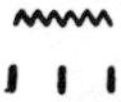	N
„	2.	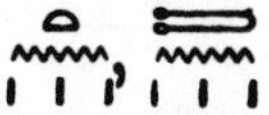	TEN, θEN
„	3.	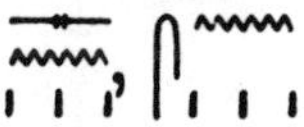	SEN

The following examples illustrate their use :—

	*ba-å*	my soul
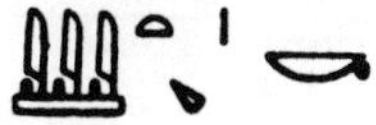	*seχet-k*	thy field

	*emmā-t*	with thee
	*ṡuit-f*	his shade
	*meṭet-s*	her words
	*ȧ teṭ en-n*	what was said by us
	*nut-ten*	your cities
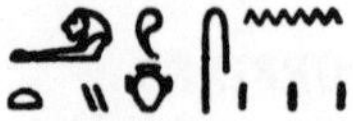	*ḥāti-sen*	their heart.

These suffixes, in the singular, when following a word indicating the noun in the dual, have the dual ending  *i* added to them; thus  *merti-fi* "his two eyes";  *muti-fi* "his two serpent mothers"; 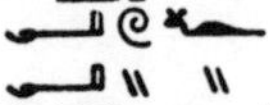 *āui-fi* "his two arms";   *reṭui-fi* "his two legs".

The forms of the pronouns are :—

I.	Sing. 1.		UȦ
	„ 2. m.	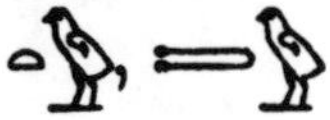	TU, ΘU
	„ 3. m.		SU
	„ 3. f.	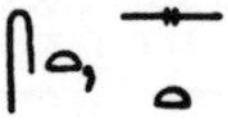	SET
	Plur. 1.		N
	„ 2.	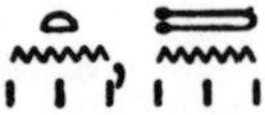	TEN, ΘEN
	„ 3.	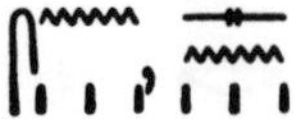	SEN

II Sing. 1. 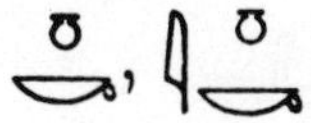 NUK, ÅNUK

" 2. m.  ENTEK, ENTUK

" 2. f. 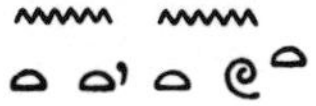 ENTET, ENTUT

" 3. m.  ENTEF, ENTUF

" 3. f.  ENTES, ENTUS.

Plur. 1. (wanting)

" 2.  ENTETEN, ENTUTEN

" 3. 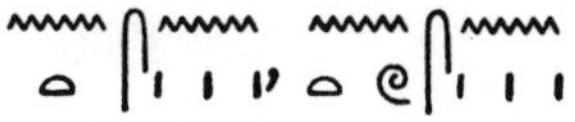 ENTESEN, ENTUSEN.

The following are examples of the use of some of these :—

1. 

ånuk *paik* *sen* *šeråu*

I thy brother younger.

2. 

ås *ben* *ånuk* *taik* *muθ*

Behold, not [am] I thy mother?

3. 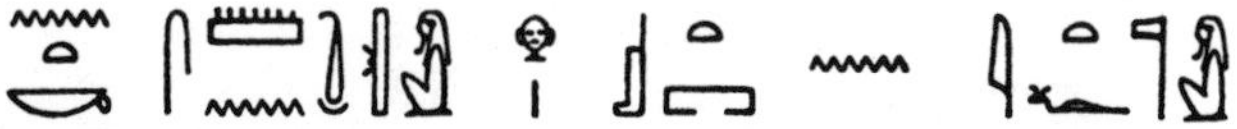

entek *smen* *ḥer* *åuset* *en* *åtef*

Thou [art] stablished upon the seat of the divine father.

4. 

entef *seśem* - *và*
He leadeth me.

5. 

teṭ *en* *sen* *àn* *ḥen-f* *entuten* *àχ*
Said to them his majesty, ye [are] what?

The demonstrative pronouns are :—

Sing.	m.		PEN	this
"	f.		TEN	this
"	m.		PEF, PEFA	that
"	f.		TEF, TEFA	that
"	m.		PA	this
"	f.		TA	this.
Plur.	m.		ÀPEN, PEN	these
"	f.	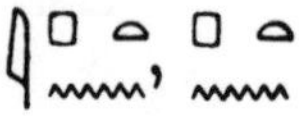	ÀPTEN, PETEN	these
"			NEFA	those
"			NA	these
"			PAU	these.

The following are examples of the use of these :—

1. 

ḥenā *àp* *pen*

With messenger this.

2. 

ḥes - sen *em* *ḥetu* *nu* *sāt* (?) *ten*

They shall recite the chapters of book this.

3. 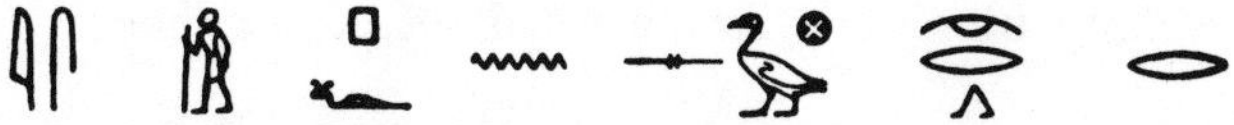

às *ser* *pef* *en* *Sa* *sper* *er*

Behold, prince that of Sais went forth to

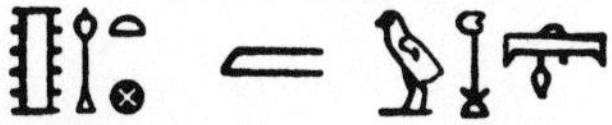

Àneb-ḥetet *em* *uχa*

Memphis in the night.

4. 

às *pefa* *pu* *teṭ* *en* *setem*

Behold, that which is said to the listener[s].

5. 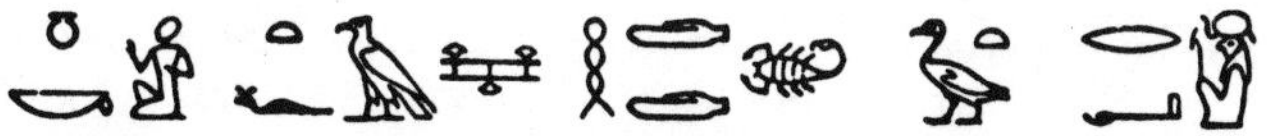

nuk *tefa* *ḥeṭeṭ* *sat* *Rā*

I [am] that scorpion the daughter of Rā.

6. 

àmmā - tu àmu-à en ta

Grant thou that I may eat the

maāst en pai àḥ

liver of this ox.

7. 

erṭā - nà ḥekau àpen

May be given to me words of power these.

8. 

àn āq qemtu - k em

Not shall enter thy disasters into

āt - à àpten

my members these.

9. 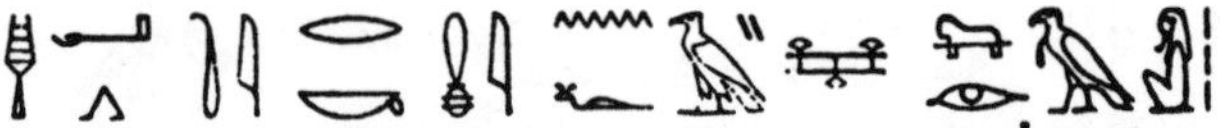

āḥā - θà erek mà nefa Ȧsàrtiu

Thou art standing like these divine Osiris beings.

10. 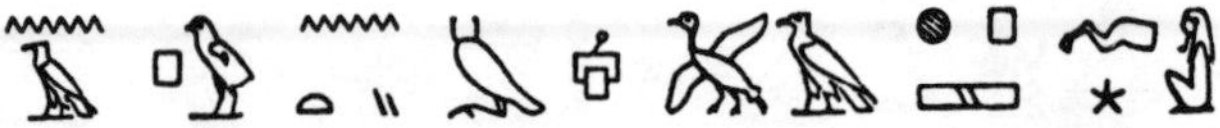

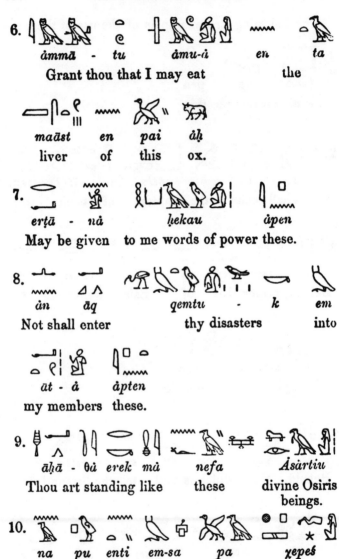

na pu enti em-sa pa χepeš

These are who [are] behind the Thigh.

11. 

pau *setem* *en* *neteru*
.....these heard of the gods.

Other words for "this" are 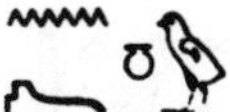 *ennu*, and , , or  *enen*, and they are used thus:—

1. 

ennu *ennui* *en* *pet*
This canal of heaven.

2. 

ṭā - k *maa-à* *enen* *χeper*
Grant thou [that] I may see this [which] happeneth

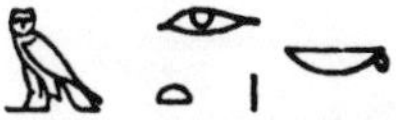

em *maat - k*
in thine eye.

The relative pronouns are  *à* and  *ent*, or  *enti* or  *entet*, and they are used thus:—

1. 

χu *θenru* *āšt* *à*
Glorious things [and] mighty deeds many which

àri-f *em* *suten*
he did as king.

2. 

àu ementuf à àri-tu nef ḥebsu

It was he who made for him clothes.

3. 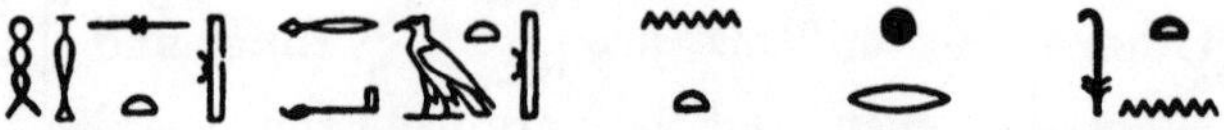

ḥest āat ent χer suten

Favour great which [he had] with the king.

4. 

àrit-nef àput neb enti em seχet

He did errand every which [was] in the fields.

5. 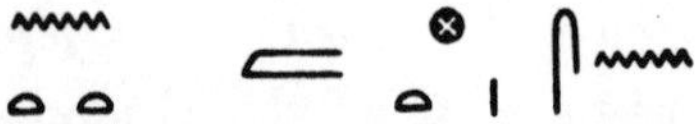

entet em nut - sen

Which [was] in city their.

The reflexive pronouns are formed by adding the word  *tes* to the pronominal suffixes thus :—

 *tes-à* myself

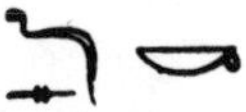 *tes-k* thyself

 *tes-t* thyself (fem.)

 *tes-f* himself

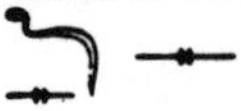 *tes-s* herself

 *tes-sen* themselves.

Examples of the use of these are :—

1. 

i - nȧ net-ȧ ṭet-ȧ ṭes-ȧ

I have come, and I have avenged my body my own.

2. 

suṭa - kuȧ mȧ suṭa - k

I have made myself strong as thou hast made

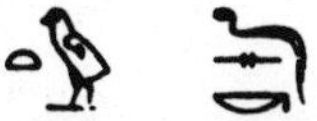

tu ṭes-k

strong thyself.

3. 

em ān neter ṭesef

In the writing of the god himself.

4. 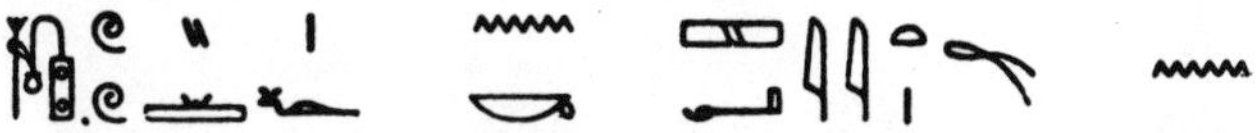

ānuu - f nek šāit en

He writeth for thee the Book of

sensen em ṭebāu-f ṭesef

Breathings with his fingers his own.

5. 

ṭeṭ ta netert em re - s ṭes - s

Speaketh the goddess with her mouth her own.

6. 

χer - sen ḥer ḥrȧ - sen em ta

They fall down upon face their . . . . in land

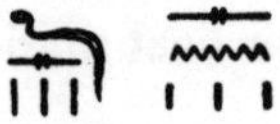

ṭes - sen

heir own.

CHAPTER VI.

NOUNS.

Nouns in Egyptian are either masculine or feminine. Masculine nouns end in U, though this characteristic letter is usually omitted by the scribe, and feminine nouns end in T. Examples of the masculine nouns are :—

 or 	*hru*	day
	*ānu*	scribe
	*ḳerḥu*	night,

but these words are just as often written ,  and 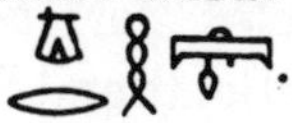. Other examples are :—

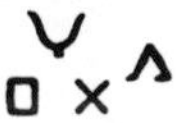	*àp*	envoy
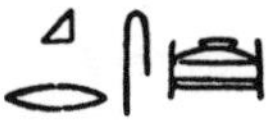	*qeres*	sepulchre
	*neter*	god
	*re*	chapter, mouth.

Examples of feminine nouns are :—

	*śāt*	book
	*pet*	heaven
	*seχet*	field
	*sebχet*	pylon
	*netert*	goddess
	*ṭept*	boat.

Masculine nouns in the plural end in U or IU, and feminine nouns in the plural in UT, but often the T is not written; examples are :—

	*ānχiu*	living beings
	*āśemu*	the forms in which the gods appear
	*ḥau*	people who live in the Delta.
	*sbau*	doors
	*suteniu netiu* (or *bȧtiu*)	Kings of the South and North
	*ḥemut*	women
	*satut*	daughters
	*meḥut*	offerings
	*ȧsut*	places.

The oldest way of expressing the plural is by writing the ideograph or picture sign three times, as the following examples taken from early texts will shew:—

 *reṭ* legs

 *χu* spirits

 *per* houses, habitations

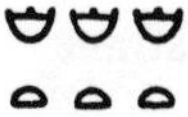 *ḥemut* women

 *nut* cities

 *seχet* fields

 *uat* ways, roads.

Sometimes the picture sign is written once with three dots, ⁝ or ooo, placed after it thus:—

 *χu* spirits

The three dots or circles ⁝ afterwards became modified into ⁞ or ǀǀǀ, and so became the common sign of the plural.

Words spelt in full with alphabetic or syllabic signs are also followed at times by ⁝:—

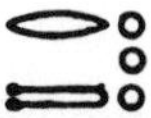 *reθ* men

 *ḥunut* young women

	*urȧu*	great ones
	*šerru*	little ones.

The plural is also expressed in the earliest times by writing the word in alphabetic or syllabic signs followed by the determinative written thrice :—

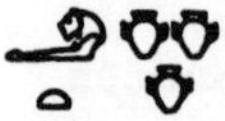	*ḥāt*	hearts
	*besek*	intestines
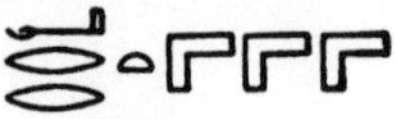	*ārrt*	abodes
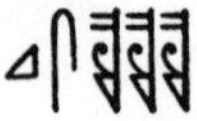	*qesu*	bones
	*seteb*	obstacles
	*ermen*	arms
	*ȧχemu-seku*	a class of stars
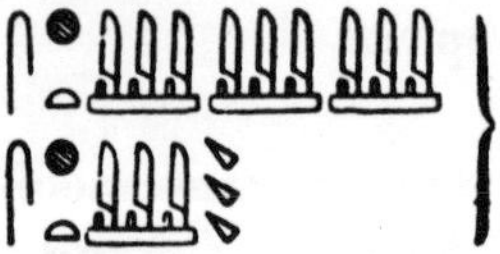	*seχet*	fields
	*seb*	stars
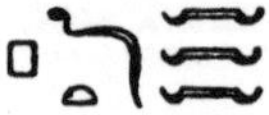	*peṭet*	bows
	*ṭām*	sceptres.

In the oldest texts the dual is usually expressed by adding UI or TI to the noun, or by doubling the picture sign thus :— the two eyes, the two ears, the two hands, the two lips, and the like. Frequently the word is spelt alphabetically or syllabically and is determined by the double picture sign, thus :—

 the two divine souls

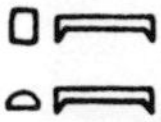 the double heaven, *i. e.*, North and South

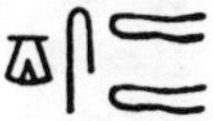 the two sides

 the two lights.

Instead of the repetition of the picture sign two strokes, ǀǀ were added to express the dual, thus *Ḥāp*, the double Nile-god. But in later times the two strokes were confused with \\, which has the value of I, and the word is also written ; but in each case the reading is *Ḥāpui*. The following are examples of the use of the dual :—

1. 

årit - nef teχenui urui em mat

He made two obelisks great of granite

2. 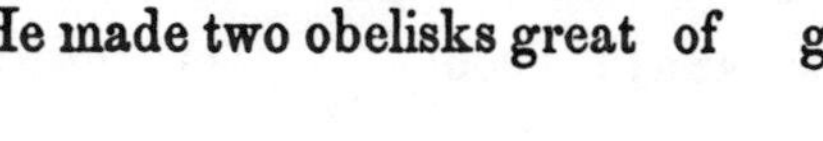

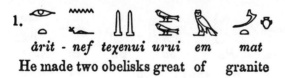

pa teχenui urui

The two obelisks great.

3. 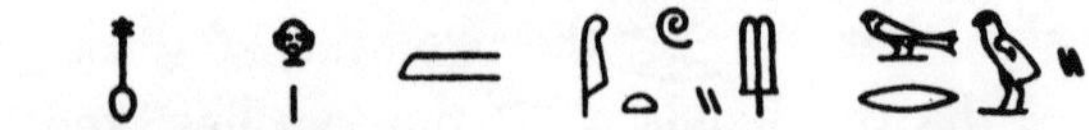

nefer ḥrȧ em šuti urui

Beautiful of face with two plumes great.

4. 

er ȧmtu beχenti urti

Between the two pylons great.

5. 

Baui-fi pui en ȧmu Ṭeṭet

His double soul that which [is] in Tattu (Busiris).

6. 

baui ḥer-ȧb ṭafui

The divine souls within the two divine Tchafui.

7. 

baui-fi ḥer-ȧbui ṭafui ba

His double soul within the two Tchafui [are] the soul

pu en Rā ba pu en Ȧsȧr

of Rā, [and] the soul of Osiris.

8. 

χā - kuȧ em sati - θen

I have risen as two daughters your.

9. 

ȧnet ḥrȧu-θen Reḥti Senti

Homage to you [ye] two opponents, [ye] two sisters,

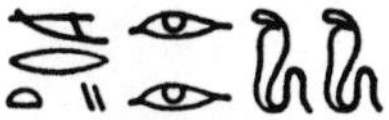

Merti

[ye] two Mert goddesses.

10. 

ṭep āui senti - k.

Upon the two hands of thy two sisters.

CHAPTER VII.

THE ARTICLE.

The definite article masculine is  or  PA, the feminine is  TA, and the plural is  NA or  NA EN; the following examples will explain the use of the article.

1. 

na *pu* *enti* *em-sa* *pa* *χepeš*

Those are who [are] behind the star Thigh

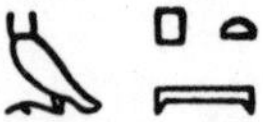

em *pet*

in heaven.

2. 

pa *bes* *en* *sešet* *ḥnā* *pa*

The flame of fire and the

uaṭ *en* *θeḥent*

tablet of crystal.

3. 

nuk pa ba en ta χat āāt

I [am] the Soul of the Body great.

4. 

reχ - kuȧ ren en pa neter

I know the name of the god[s]

XLII en uneniu ḥenā - k

forty-two who exist with thee.

5. 

nefer pa stimu em ta ȧset

Good [is] the grass in the place

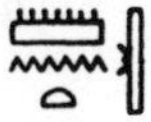

ment

such and such.

6. 

ta ḥemt en paif sen āa

The wife of his brother elder

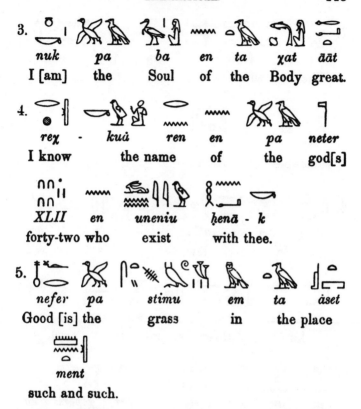

ȧu - tu ḥems ḥer nebṭ - set

she was sitting at her hair.[1]

[1] *I. e.*, she was sitting dressing her hair.

7. 

na *šeršeru* *en* *p[a]* *ȧšeṭ*

The winds (air) of the acacia tree

šeps *en* *Ȧnnu*

venerable of Ȧnnu.

8. 

ȧu-f *ḥer* *χaṭbu* *taif* *ḥemt*

He slew his wife,

ȧu-f *ḥer* *χaā - set* *na* *en* *ȧu*

he threw her [to] the dogs.

9. 

un *ȧn* *pa* *sti* .... *ḥer* *χeperu* *em*

The smell became in

na *en* *ḥebsu* *en* *Āa-perti*

the garments of Pharaoh.

The masculine indefinite article is expressed by 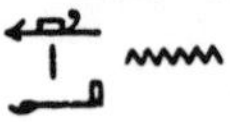 ***uā en***, and the feminine by 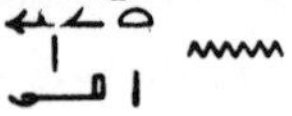 ***uāt*** *en*; the words *uā en* and *uāt en* mean, literally, "one of". Examples are :—

1. 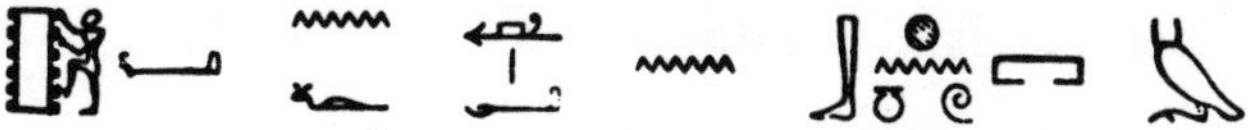

qeṭ - nef uā en beχennu em

He built a house with

ṭet - f em ta ȧnt pa āś

his own hand in the valley of the cedar.

2. 

ȧu-f ḥer ȧn uā en sfenṭ ḳeśȧ

He brought a knife [for cutting] reeds.

3. 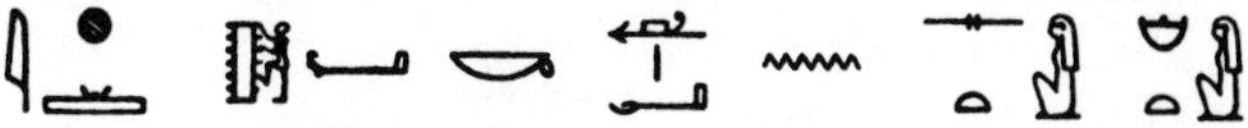

ȧχ qeṭ - k uā en set ḥemt

O fashion thou a wife

en Batau

for Batau.

4. 

χer ȧr ȧu-k qem - f emtuk

When thou findest it, thou shalt

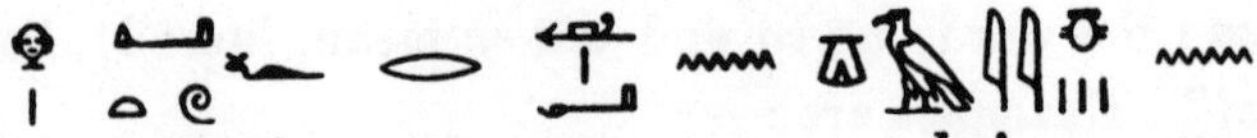

ḥer ṭātu-f er uā en ḳai en

put it into a pot of

mu qebḥ ka ānχ - à

water cold, [and] verily I shall live.

5. 

àu pa Rā ḥer ṭāt χeperu uā en

The Rā caused to become a

mu āa er àuṭ - f er àuṭ

stream great between him [and] between

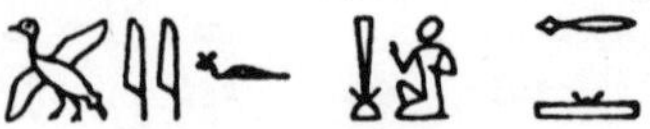

paif sen āa

his brother elder.

From the union of the definite article with the personal suffixes is formed the following series of words :—

MASCULINE.		FEMININE.	
	*pai-à*		*tai-à*

pai-k	*tai-k*
pai-t (two forms)	*tai-t*
pai-f	*tai-f*
pai-s }	*tai-s* }
pai-set }	*tai-set* }
pai-n	*tai-n*
pai-ten	*tai-ten*
pai-sen	*tai-sen*
pai-u	*tai-u*

COMMON.

nai-à	*nai-n*
nai-à	
nai-k	*nai-ten*
nai-θ }	
nai-t }	
nai-f	*nai-sen*
nai-s	*nai-u*

The following examples will illustrate their use :—

1. 

pai-ȧ sen āa ḥer sȧnnu - nȧ

My brother elder hurried me.

2. 

pai-ȧ neb nefer

My lord beautiful.

3. 

ȧχ pai - k i em-sa-ȧ er

Fie on thy coming after me to

χaṭbu

slay [me].

4. 

χer pai-t hai emmā-ȧ

For thy husband [is] to me

em seχeru en ȧtef

in the guise of a father.

5. 

ȧs ta ḥemt en pai-f sen āa

Behold the wife of his brother elder

senṭu - θȧ

was afraid.

6. 

ȧu - set ḥer teṭ en pai - set sȧu

She said to her keeper.

7. 

ȧu ḥāti - sen ḥer neṫem ḥer pai - sen

Were their hearts rejoicing over their

rā baku

doing of work.

8. 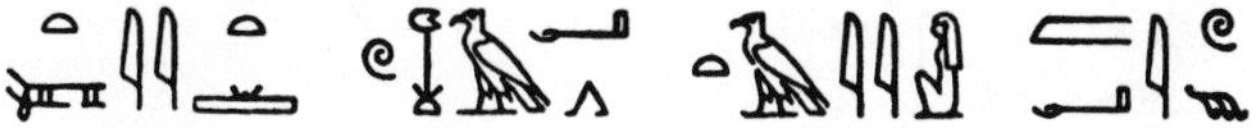

temit uχaā tai-ȧ māȧu·

That not may fall my hair

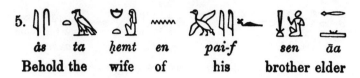

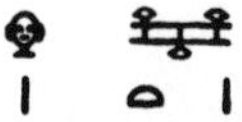

ḥer uat

on the way

9. 

tai-k *šāi* *āš-θȧ* *em* *nasaqu*

Thy letter abounds in breaks.

10. 

suten *neb* *ḥenā* *tai-u* *suten* *ḥemut*

King[s] all with their queens.

1. 

ȧmmā *ȧn-tu-nȧ* *nai-ȧ* *uru*

Let be brought to me my nobles

āaiu

great.

2. 

er *nai-k* *re-ḥet* *āaiu*

To thy storehouses great

em *Uast*

in Thebes.

3. 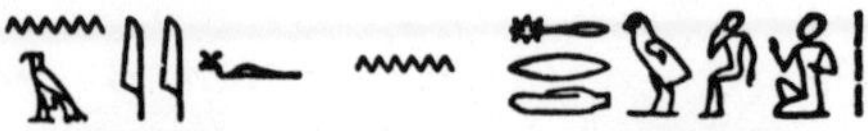

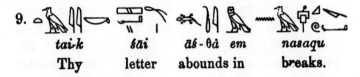

nai-f *en* *χarṭu*

His children.

4. 

χer nai - sen χāi en rā āś-

With their weapons, numerous

set em śā

were they as the sand.

5. 

nai-u qerȧu em χemt

Their bolts of copper (*or* bronze).

6. 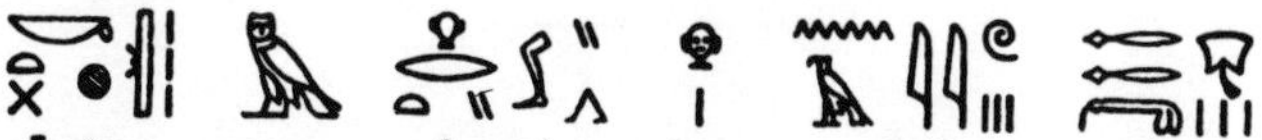

keteχ em ḥerti ḥer naiu āā

Goods on porter[s] and upon their asses.

7. 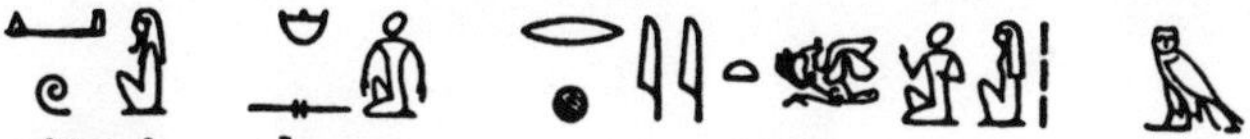

ṭāu-ȧ ḥems reχit em

I caused to sit the people in

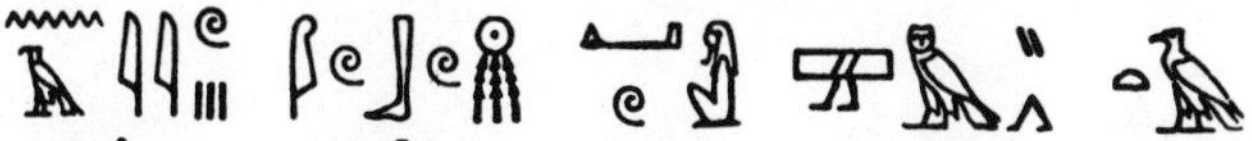

nai-u qubu ṭāu-ȧ śemi ta

their shadow. I caused to travel the

set Ta-merȧ itu - s seuseχ-θ

woman of Egypt on her journey making long [her journey]

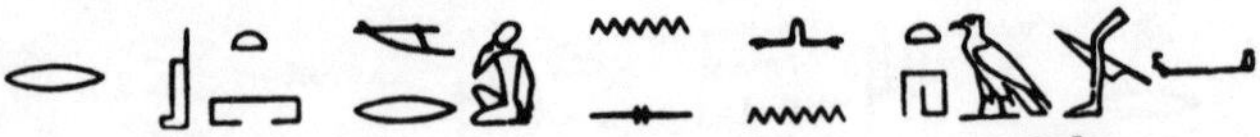

er *àset* *mer - nes* *àn* *teha-*

to the place she wished [to go], not attacked

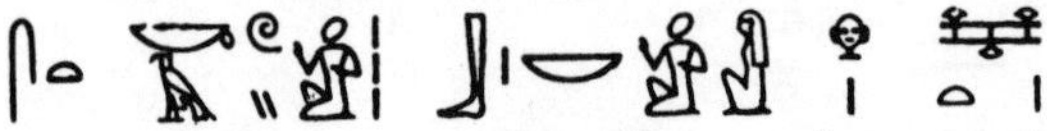

set *kaui* *bu-nebu* *ḥer* *uat*

her any person whatsoever on the way

CHAPTER VIII.

ADJECTIVES, NUMERALS, TIME, THE YEAR, ETC.

The **adjective** is, in form, often similar to the noun, with which it agrees in gender and number ; with a few exceptions it comes after its noun, thus :—

χet nebt nefert ābt χet nebt neṭemet beneret
Thing every, good, pure; thing every, pleasant, sweet.

The following will explain the use of the adjective in the singular and plural.

1. 

ānχ-ȧ em tau en beti ḥeṭet
Let me live upon bread of barley white,

ḥeqet-ȧ em pertu ṭešeru
my ale [made] of grain red.

2. 

àu ḥen ḥer ḥems ḥer àrit hru

Was [His] Majesty sitting to make a day

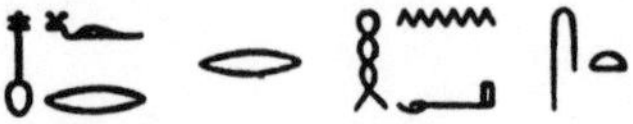

nefer er ḥenā - set

happy with her.

3. 

qem - k ta śeràu nefer

Thou didst find the girl pretty

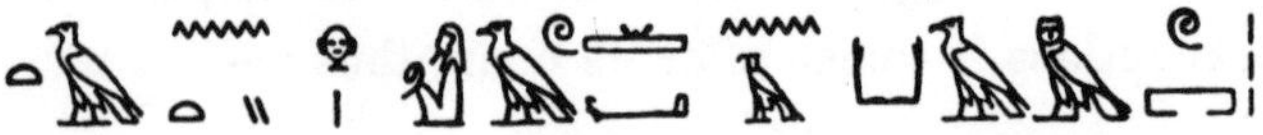

ta enti ḥer sau na kamu

who was watching the gardens.

4. 

ka àri-à nek ḥebsu neferu

Indeed I will make for thee clothes beautiful.

5. 

àu - sen ḥer ruṭ em śauabu

They grew into trees

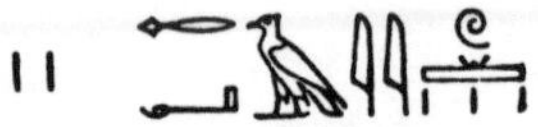

sen āaiu

two great.

6. 

àu-à *em-baḥ* *neteru* *āaiu*

I am in the presence of the gods great.

The adjectives "royal" and "divine" are usually written before the noun, thus :—

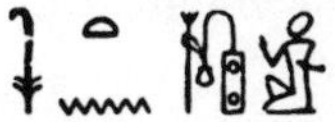	*suten ān*	royal scribe
	*suten ḥemu*	royal workman
	*suten uaà*	royal boat *or* barge
	*suten reχ*	royal acquaintance *or* kinsman
	*suten ḥemt*	royal woman, *i. e.*, queen
	*sutenu ḥenu*	royal servants
	*neter ḥen*	divine servant, *i. e.*, priest
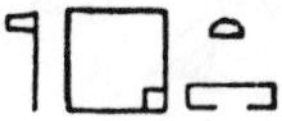	*neter ḥet*	divine house, *i. e.*, temple
	*neter àtef*	divine father.

Adjectives are without degrees of comparison in Egyptian, but the comparative and superlative may be expressed in the following manner :—

1. 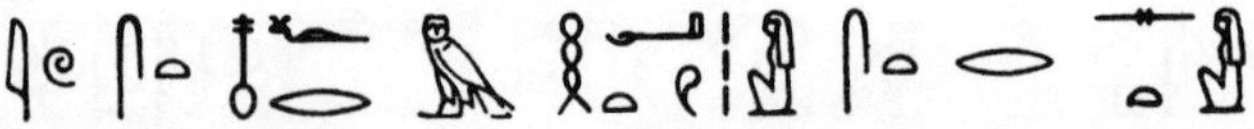

àu - set nefer em ḥāt - set er set

She was fair in her body more than

ḥemt nebt enti em pa ta ṭer - f

woman any who [was] in the earth the whole of it.

2. 

ur - k er neteru

Great art thou more than the gods.

3. 

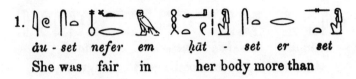

se - āšt - u er šā

They were numerous more than the sand.

4. 

ànet ḥrà - k χu er neteru

Homage to thee [O thou one] glorious more than the gods.

5. 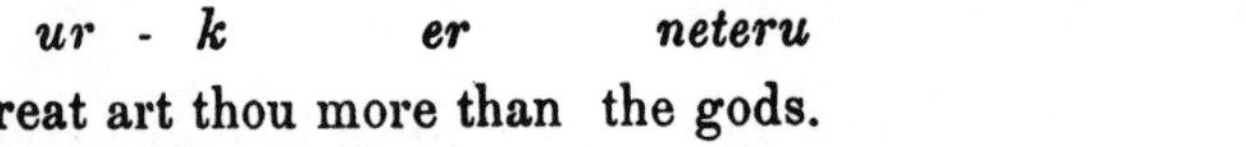

betenu er θesemu χaχet

Fleet more than greyhounds, swift

er šuit

more than light.

6. 

χeper · *àqer - k* · *eref* · *em*

It shall happen thou shalt be wise more than he by

ḳer

being silent.

7. 

nefer · *setem* · *er* · *entet* · *neb*

Good is hearkening more than anything, *i. e.*, to obey is best of all.

Numerals.

I	=		*uā*	=	1
II	=		*sen*	=	2
III	=		*χemet*	=	3
IIII	=	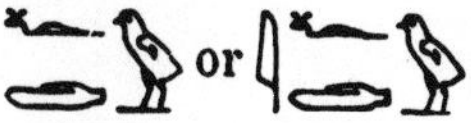	*fṭu* or *àfṭu*	=	4
II III ★	=		*ṭuau*	=	5
III III	=		*sàs*	=	6
III IIII	=		*sefeχ*	=	7

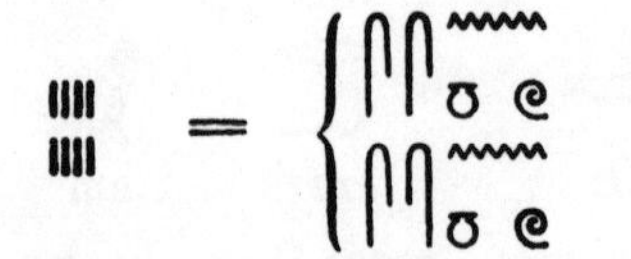	*χemennu*	=	8
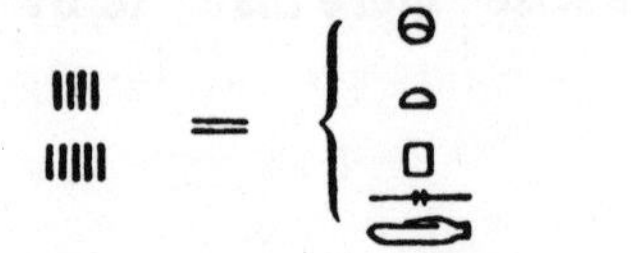	*pesṭ*	=	9
	*met*	=	10
	*ṭaut*	=	20
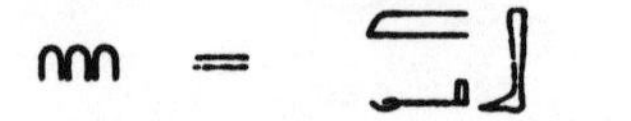	*māb*	=	30
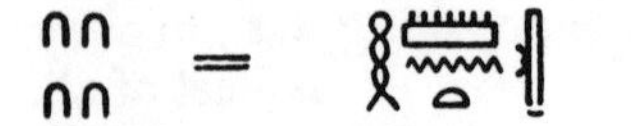	*ḥement*	=	40
 = (?)	(?)	=	50
 = (?)	(?)	=	60
	*sefeχ*	=	70
	*χemennui*	=	80
 = (?)	(?)	=	90
	*śaā*	=	100
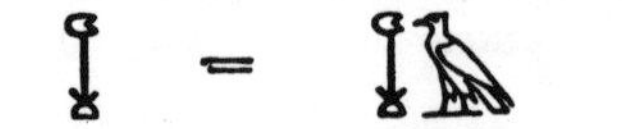	*χa*	=	1000
	*ṭāb*	=	10,000
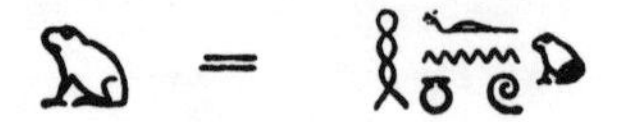	*ḥefennu*	=	100,000

𓁨 = 𓎛𓎛𓁨 *ḥeḥ* = 1,000,000

𓍶 = 𓍶𓈖𓏌𓅱 *šennu* = 10,000,000

The ordinals are formed by adding 𓏌 *nu* to the numeral, with the exception of "first", thus :—

	Masc.		Fem.	
First	𓁶𓊪𓏭	*ṭepi*	𓁶𓊪𓏏	*ṭept*
Second	𓏻𓏌		𓏻𓏌𓏏	
Third	𓏼𓏌		𓏼𓏌𓏏	
Fourth	𓏽𓏌		𓏽𓏌𓏏	
Fifth	𓏾𓏌		𓏾𓏌𓏏	
Sixth	𓏿𓏌		𓏿𓏌𓏏	
Seventh	𓐀𓏌		𓐀𓏌𓏏	
Eighth	𓐁𓏌		𓐁𓏌𓏏	
Ninth	𓐂𓏌		𓐂𓏌𓏏	
Tenth	𓎆𓏌		𓎆𓏌𓏏	

and so on. From the following examples of the use of the numerals it will be noticed that the numeral, like the adjective, is placed *after* the noun, that the lesser numeral comes last, and that the noun is sometimes in the singular and sometimes in the plural.

1. 

reχ - kuȧ ren en pa neter XLII

I know the name of the god forty-two, *i. e.*, I know the names of the forty-two gods.

2. 

re en tekau IV

Chapter of the flames four, *i. e.*, "four flames".

3. 

nes su χet 300 em au-f

Belong to him measure[s] 300 in his length,

χet 230 em useχt-f

measure[s] 230 in his breadth.

4. 

meḥ 1000 pu em au-f

Cubit[s] one thousand is he in his length.

5. 

ṭāu-ȧ nek met en ṭebā en ṭep en

I have given to thee { 10 of 10,000 *i. e.*, tens of ten thousands } of bushels of

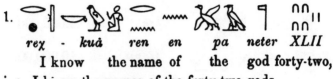

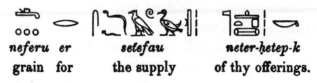

neferu er seṭefau neter-ḥetep-k

grain for the supply of thy offerings.

6. 

āqu *āaiu* $(100,000 \times 9) + (10,000 \times 9)$

Loaves large, 900,000 + 90,000

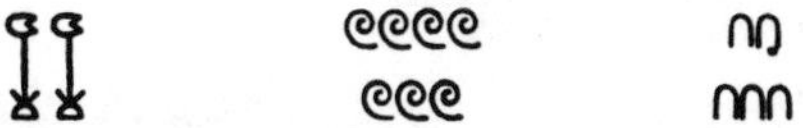

$+ (1000 \times 2) + (100 \times 7) + (10 \times 5)$

+ 2000 + 700 + 50

i. e., 992,750 large loaves of bread.

7. In the papyrus of Rameses III we have the following numbers of various kinds of geese set out and added up thus :—

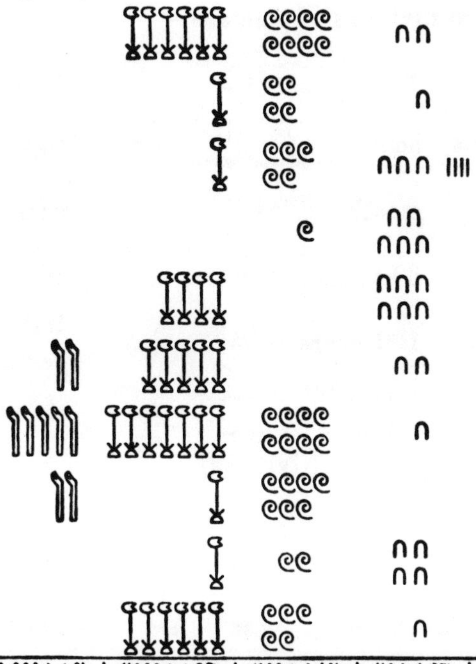

= 6820

= 1410

= 1534

= 150

= 4060

= 25020

= 57810

= 21700

= 1240

= 6510

Total $(10,000 \times 9) + (1000 \times 32) + (100 \times 40) + (10 \times 25) + 4 = 126,254$

Ordinal numbers are also indicated by  *meḥ*, which is placed before the figure thus :—

1. 

em	*maāu*	*meḥ*	*uā*	*em*	*maāu*
In	the temples	of the	first [rank],	in	the temples

meḥ	*sen*

of the second [rank].

Time.

The principal divisions of time are :—

	*ḥat*	second		*at*	minute
	*unnut*	hour	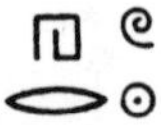	*hru*	day
	*ȧbeṭ*	month		*renpit*	year
	*seṭ*	30 years		*ḥen*	60 years
	*ḥenti*	120 years		*ḥeḥ*	100,000 years
	*ḥeḥ*	1,000,000 years		*ṭetta*	eternity.

 *sen* 10,000,000

Examples of the use of these are :—

1. 

ṭā - f	*renput*	*āšt*	*ḥer*	*ḥer*	*renput-ȧ*
May he give	years	many	over	and above	my years

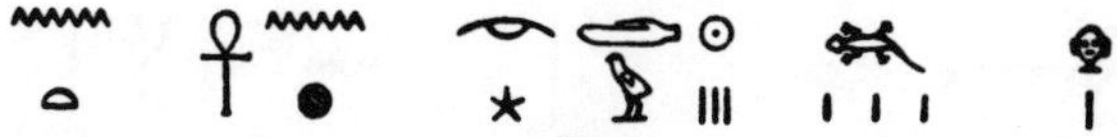

ent ānχ åbeṭu āš ḥer

of life; [and] months many {over, *i. e.*, in addition to}

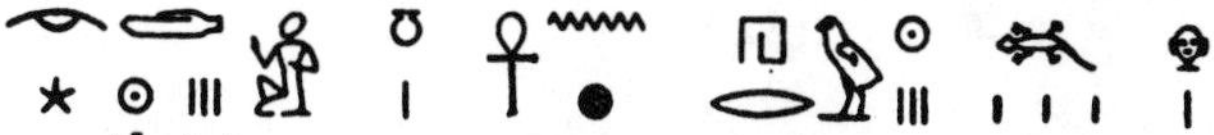

åbet-å nu ānχ hru āš ḥer

my months of life; [and] days many over

hru-å nu ānχ ḳerḥ āš ḥer

my days of life; [and] nights many over

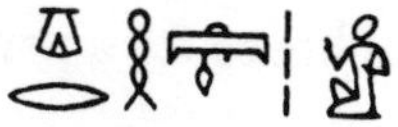

ḳerḥ - å

my nights.

2. 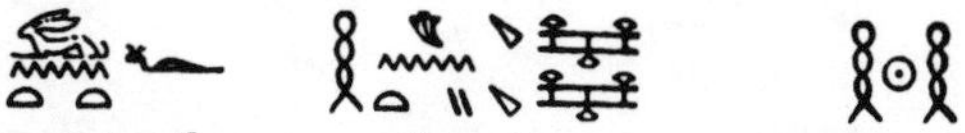

untet - f ḥenti ḥeḥ

His existence is [for] 120 years × 100,000 years.

3. 

uneniu ānχ er neḥeḥ ḥenti

Who exist living for ever, 120 years ×

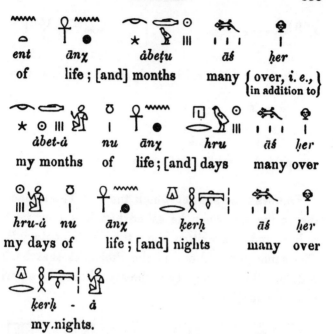

ṭetta

eternity.

4. 

ȧu - k *er* *ḥeḥ* *en* *ḥeḥ*

Thou art for millions of years of millions of years,

āḥā *ḥeḥ*

a period of millions of years.

This was the answer which the god Thoth made to the scribe Ani when he asked him how long he had to live, and was written about the XVIth century B. C. The same god told one of the Ptolemies that he had ordained the sovereignty of the royal house for a period of time equal to :—

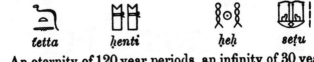

ṭetta *ḥenti* *ḥeḥ* *seṭu*

An eternity of 120 year periods, an infinity of 30 year periods,

ḥeḥ *renput* *šenu ȧbeṭ* *ḥefnu*

millions of years, ten millions of months, hundreds of thousands

hru *ṭebāu* *unnut* *χau* *at*

of days, tens of thousands of hours, thousands of minutes,

śaā *ḥat* *met* *ȧnt*

hundreds of seconds, [and] tens of thirds of seconds

THE EGYPTIAN YEAR.

The year, *renpit,* plural consisted originally of twelve months, each containing thirty days; as the month contained three periods of ten days the year consisted of thirty-six weeks of ten days each. Later the Egyptians added five days[1] to the years, and thus made it equal to 365 days .[2] Each month was dedicated to a god. The twelve months were divided into three seasons of four months each, thus:—

1. *akhet* season of inundation and period of sowing.
2. *pert* season of "coming forth" or growing, *i.e.*, spring.
3. *śemut* season of harvest and beginning of inundation.

Documents were dated thus:—

[1] Called "epagomenal days".

[2] They discovered that the true year was longer than 365 days, that the difference between 365 days and the length of the true year was equal nearly to one day in four years, and that New Year's day ran through the whole year in 365 × 4 = 1460 years.

1. 

renpit IV ȧbeṭ IV akhet hru 1

Year four, month four of the sowing season, day one

χer ḥen en

under the majesty of, etc.

i. e., the first day of the fourth month of the sowing season in the fourth year of the reign of king So-and-so.

2. 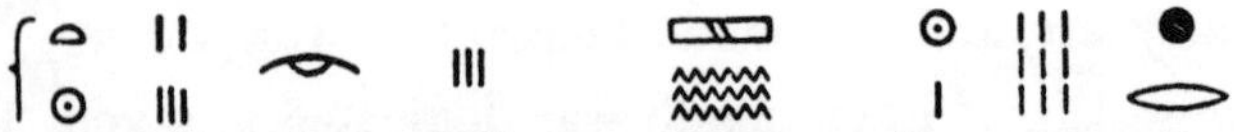

renpit V ȧbeṭ III šemut hru pesṭ χer

Year five, month three of inundation, day nine under

ḥen en suten net (or bȧt) Usr-Maāt-Rā-setep-en-Rā

the majesty of {the king of the South and North} Usr-Maāt-Rā-setep-en-Rā,

sa Rā Rā-meses-meri-Ȧmen

son of the Sun, Rameses, beloved of Amen, etc.

3. 

renpit XXI ȧbeṭ I akhet χer

Year twenty-one, month one of sowing season under

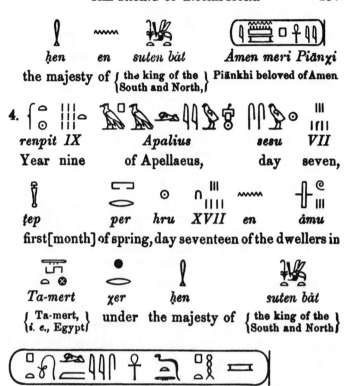

ḥen en suten bȧt Ȧmen meri Piānχi

the majesty of {the king of the South and North,} Piānkhi beloved of Amen

4. 

renpit IX Apalius sesu VII

Year nine of Apellaeus, day seven,

ṭep per hru XVII en ȧmu

first [month] of spring, day seventeen of the dwellers in

Ta-mert χer ḥen suten bȧt

{Ta-mert, *i. e.,* Egypt} under the majesty of {the king of the South and North}

Ptualmis ānχ ṭetta Ptaḥ meri

Ptolemy, living for ever, beloved of Ptah.

This date shews that there was a difference of ten days between the dating in use among the priests and that of the Egyptians in the time of Ptolemy III Euergetes, king of Egypt from B. C. 247 to B. C. 222.

4. 

renpit XXXII ȧbeṭ III šemut hru VI

Year thirty-two, month three of sowing season, day six

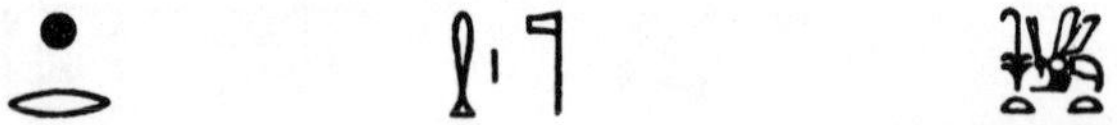

χer *ḥen* *suten bȧt*
under the divine majesty of {the king of the South and North,}

Rā-usr-maāt - meri - Ȧmen *ānχ* *uta*
Rā-usr-maāt - meri - Amen, life! strength!

senb *sa Rā* *Rāmeses* *ḥeq Ȧnnu*
health! son of the Sun, Rameses, prince of Heliopolis.

The words 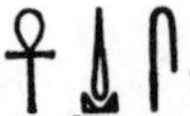, which frequently follow royal names, may be also translated "Life to him! Strength to him! Health to him!" They often occur after any mention of or reference to the king, thus :—

1. 

pa *θȧireȧa* *āa* *en* *Āa-perti*
The door great of Pharaoh,

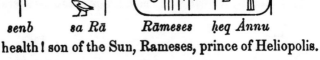

ānχ *uta* *senb*
life! strength! health!

2. 

uā en suten ḥemu ṭep en ḥen - f

One royal workman first of His Majesty,

ānχ uṭa senb

life! strength! health!

It has been said above that each month was dedicated to a god, and it must be noted that the month was called after the god's name. The Copts or Egyptian Christians have preserved, in a corrupt form, the old Egyptian names of the months, which they arrange in the following order:—

1st month of winter		=	Thoth
2nd „	„	=	Paopi
3rd „	„	=	Hathor
4th „	„	=	Khoiak
1st month of spring		=	Tobi
2nd „	„	=	Mekhir
3rd „	„	=	Phamenoth
4th „	„	=	Pharmuthi

	1st month of summer	=	Pakhon
 „	2nd „ „	=	Paoni
 „	3rd „ „	=	Epep
 „	4th „ „	=	Mesore.

The epagomenal days were called  "the five days over (*i. e.*, to be added to) the year".

CHAPTER IX.

THE VERB.

The consideration of the Egyptian verb, or stem-word, is a difficult subject, and one which can only be properly illustrated by a large number of extracts from texts of all periods. Egyptologists have, moreover, agreed neither as to the manner in which it should be treated, nor as to the classification of the forms which have been distinguished. The older generation of scholars were undecided as to the class of languages under which the Egyptian language should be placed, and contented themselves with pointing out grammatical forms analogous to those in Coptic, and perhaps in some of the Semitic dialects; but recently the relationship of Egyptian to the Semitic languages has been boldly affirmed, and as a result the nomenclature of the Semitic verb or stem-word has been applied to that of Egyptian.

The Egyptian stem-word may be indifferently a verb or a noun; thus  *χeper* means "to be, to become", and the "thing which has come into being". By the addition of  the stem-word obtains a participial meaning like "being" or "becoming"; by the addition of  in the masc. and 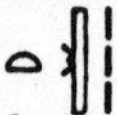 in the fem. *χeper* becomes a noun in the plural meaning "things which exist", "created things", and the like; and by the addition of  we have  *χeperȧ* the god to whom the property of creating men and things belonged. The following examples will illustrate the various uses of the word:—

1. 

neter *uāu* *χeper* *em* *sep* *ṭep*

The god one [who] came into being in time primeval.

2. 

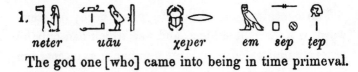

χeper *meṭet* *nebt* *Tem*

Came into being words all of Tem.

3. 

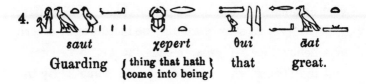

ȧn *χepert* *sat* *ṭu*

Not had come into being earth [and] mountains.

4. 

saut *χepert* *θui* *āat*

Guarding {thing that hath come into being} that great.

5. 

ȧri-ȧ *χeperu* *neb* *er* *ṭāṭā*

I have made transformations all at the dictates

ȧb-ȧ *em* *bu* *neb* *mer* *ka-ȧ*

of my heart in place every [which] wished my *ka*.

6. 

em *ḥrȧ* *en* *χeperu* *ḥā* *i - ḥer - sa*

In the face of men and women and those who shall come

sen

after them.

7. 

ȧn *reχ - en - tu* *χepert* *ȧrit*

Not are known {the things that will come into being} [as] the work

neter

of God.

8. 

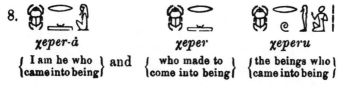

χeper-ȧ *χeper* *χeperu*

{I am he who came into being} and {who made to come into being} {the beings who came into being}

χeperu - *kuȧ* *em* *χeperu* *en*
I came into being in the forms of

χeperȧ *χeper* *em* *sep* *ṭepi*
the god Khepera, who came into being in primeval time.

Or again, if we take a word like  *ȧqer* it will be seen from the following examples that according to its position and use in a sentence it becomes a noun, or a verb, or an adjective, or an adverb.

1. 

sma-ȧ *em* *χu* *śepsi* *ȧqer*
May I join the spirits holy [and] perfect

nu *neter-χert*
of the underworld.

2. 

śāt (?) *ent* *sȧqer* *χu*
The book of making {perfect or strong} {the spirit [of the deceased].}

3. 

ȧu-f *netri* *emmā* *ȧqeru*
He is divine among the perfect ones.

4. 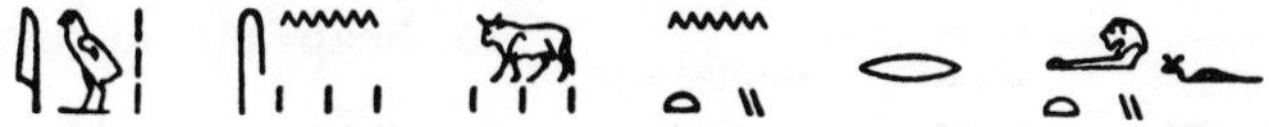

ȧu - sen ȧaut enti er - ḥāti-f

They, the cattle which were before him

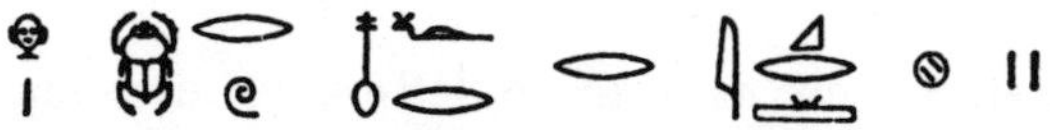

ḥer χeperu nefer er ȧqer sep sen

became fine, exceedingly, twice.

I. e., the cattle became very fine indeed.

Stem-words in Egyptian, like those in Hebrew and other Semitic dialects, consist of two, three, four, and five letters, which are usually consonants, one or more of which may be vowels, as examples of which may be cited :—

	*ān*	to return, go or send back
	*ha*	to walk
	*āḥā*	to stand
	*šāṭ*	to cut
	*rerem*	to weep
	*neḳa*	to cut
	*nemmes*	to enlighten
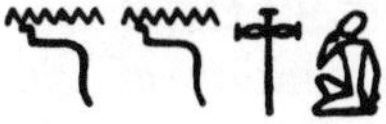	*netnet*	to converse

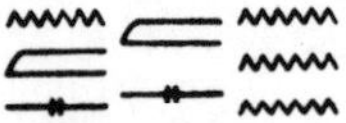	*nemesmes*	to heap up to overflowing.
	*nefemnefem*	(probably pronounced *nefemfem*) to love.

The stem-words with three letters or consonants, which are ordinarily regarded as triliteral roots, may be reduced to two consonants, which were pronounced by the help of some vowel between ; these we may call primary or biliteral roots. Originally all roots consisted of one syllable. By the addition of feeble consonants in the middle or at the end of the monosyllabic root, or by repeating the second consonant, roots of three letters were formed. Roots of four consonants are formed by adding a fourth consonant, or by combining two roots of two letters ; and roots of five consonants from two triliteral roots by the omission of one consonant.

Speaking generally, the Egyptian verb has no conjugation or species like Hebrew and the other Semitic dialects, and no Perfect (Preterite) or Imperfect (Future) tenses. The exact pronunciation of a great many verbs must always remain unknown, because the Egyptians never invented a system of vocalisation, and never took the trouble to indicate the various vowel sounds like the Syrians and Arabs ; but by comparing forms which are common both to Egyptian and Coptic, a tolerably correct idea of the pronunciation may be obtained.

There is in Egyptian a derivative formation of the

word-stem or verb, which is made by the addition of S, —— or ∩, to the simple form of the verb, and which has a causative signification; in Coptic the causative is expressed both by a prefixed S and T. The following are examples of the use of the Egyptian causative:—

1. From  *āa* to be great:—

s-āa-à *neferu-f*

I made great, *i. e.*, magnified his beauties.

2. From  *ānχ* to live:—

àtḥu-à *mennu* *āaiu* *mà* *ṭuu*

I dragged [two] statues huge as mountains

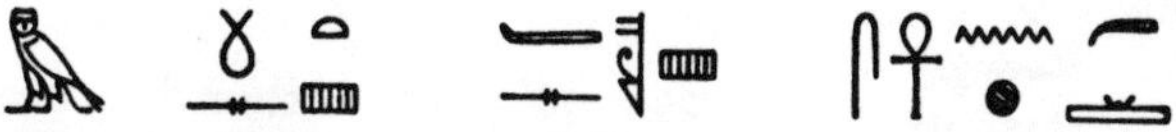

em *śeset* *beḥes* *s-ānχ*

of white marble [and] alabaster, and I made [them] like life

em *àri* *ḥetep* *ḥer* *unemet* *semḥi*

making [them] to rest at the right [and] left

en *pai - s* *reàt* *χeti*

of its door inscribed

ḥer *ren* *ur* *ḥen - k*

with the name great of thy majesty.

3. From  *χeper* to become :—

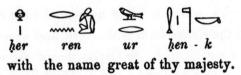

seχeperu - *nȧ* *re-ḥetu-f*

I made to come into being his treasure-houses

bāḥ *em* *χet* *ta* *neb*

[which were] flooded with things of every land.

The verb with pronominal personal suffixes is as follows :—

Sing. 1 com.		*reχ-ȧ*	I know
2 m.		*neḥem-k*	thou deliverest
2 f.		*teṭ-t*	thou speakest
3 m.		*šāṭ-f*	he cuts
3 f.		*qem-s*	she finds
Plur. 1 com.		*ȧri-n*	we do
2 com.		*mit-ten*	ye die
3 com.		*χeper-sen*	they become.

The commonest **auxiliary verbs** are *āḥā* to stand; *un* to be; *àu* to be; *àri* to do; *ṭā* to give; the following passages illustrate their use:—

1. 

un *àn - f* *ḥer* *teṭ* *nes* *set* *āḥā*

Was he saying to her, 'Stand up

ṭā-t *nà* *pertu*

give thou to me grain'.

2. 

āḥā *teṭ - set* *nef* *bu* *pu* *uā* *meṭet*

Stood up said she to him, 'No one hath spoken

enmā-à *ḥeru* *paik* *sen* *šeràu*

with me except thy young brother'.

3. 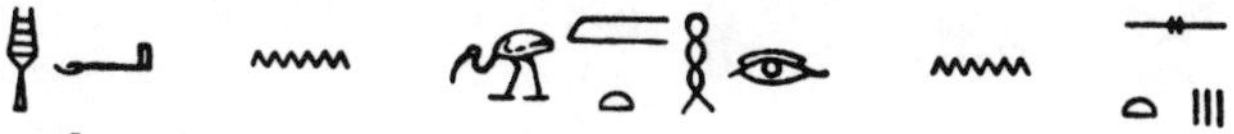

āḥā *en* *qemḥet* *en* *set*

Stood up glanced at them

ḥen - f *āḥā - nef* *χāra* *er*

His Majesty, he stood up furious with rage against

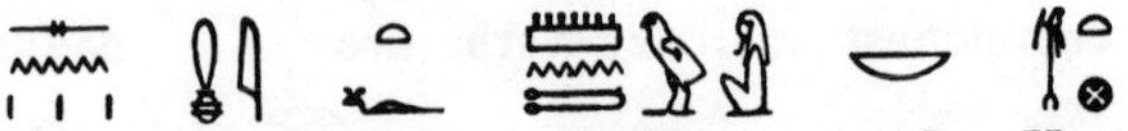

sen mȧ tef Menθu neb Uast

them like father Menthu, lord of Thebes.

1. 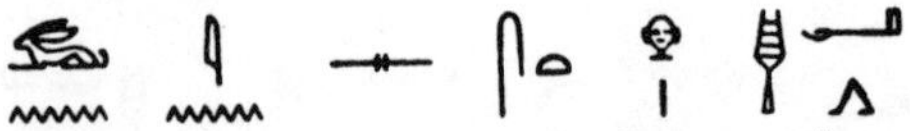

un ȧn - s set ḥer aḥā

Was she standing up.

2. 

un ȧn - f ḥer ṭeṭtu emmā - s

Was he speaking with her

set em ṭeṭ

saying :—

3. 

un ȧn - f ḥer ārqu - f en

Was he taking an oath to him by

pa Rā - Ḥeru - χuti em ṭeṭ

the god Rā - Harmachis, saying :—

4. 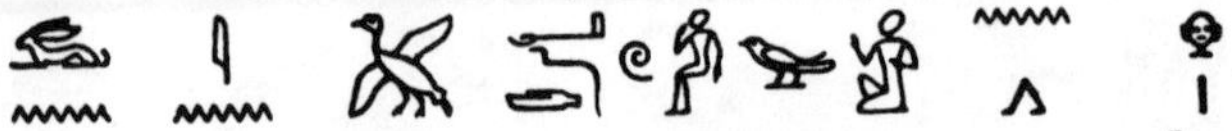

un ȧn pa āṭeṭu en ḥer

Was the young man coming (?) to

meṭu *emmā* *paif* *sen*

speak with his brother.

1. 

àu-à *sentˌ-kuà* *en* *baiu-k*

I am fearing thy souls (*i. e.*, will).

2. 

àu-f *ḥer* *sper* *er* *paif* *per*

Was he going into his house,

àu-f *ḥer* *qem* *taif* *ḥemt*

was he finding his wife

seṭer-θà *mer-θà* *en* *āṭau*

lying sick through {violent treatment.}

àu-set *ḥer* *temt* *ṭāt* *mu* *ḥer* *ṭet-f*

Was she not putting water upon his hand

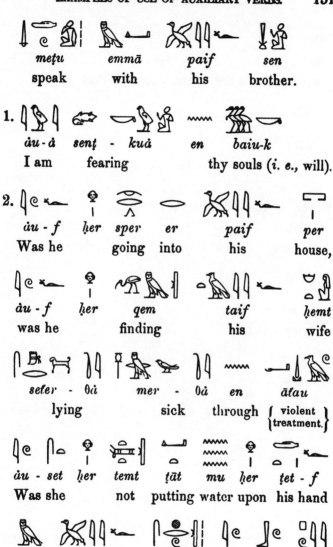

em *paif* *seχeru* *àu* *bu* *pui*

according to his wont. Was not

set setau er - ḥāt - f àu paif

she lighting a fire before him. Was his

per em kekui

house in darkness.

1. 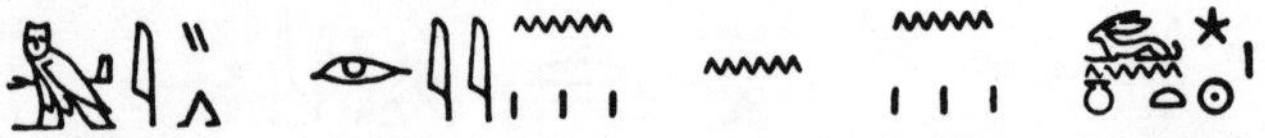

māài àri - n en - n unnut

Come, let us make for ourselves an hour

seṭeru

lying down.

2. 

em àri meḥ àb - k aχetu

[Do] not make to fill heart thy [with] the wealth

kai

of another.

1. 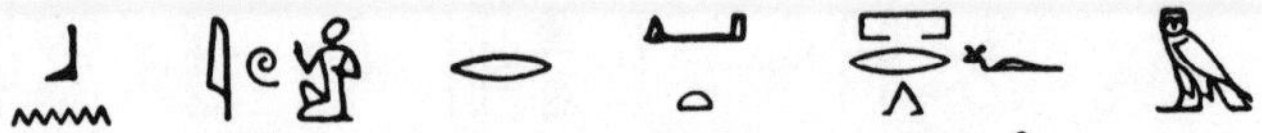

ben àu-à er ṭāt per - f em

Not am I letting to come forth it from

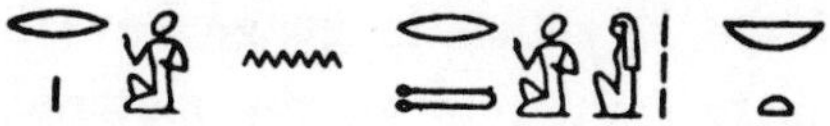

re - à *en* *reθ* *nebt*

my mouth to people any.

2. 

emtuf *àn* *naif* *àaut*

He brought his cattle

er - ḥāt - f *er* *ṭāt* *seṭer - u* *em*

before him to make lie down them in

pai - sen *àhait*

their stalls.

In the limits of this little book it is impossible to set before the reader examples of the use of the various parts of the verb, and to illustrate the forms of it which have been identified with the Infinitive and Imperative moods and with participial forms. If the Egyptian verb is to be treated as a verb in the Semitic languages we should expect to find forms corresponding to the Kal, Niphal, Piel, Pual, Hiphil, Shaphel, and other conjugations, according as we desired to place it in the Southern or Northern group of Semitic dialects. Forms undoubtedly exist which lend themselves readily to Semitic nomenclature, but until all the texts belonging to all periods of the Egyptian language have been published, that is to say, until all the material for grammatical investigation has been put into the Egyptologists' hands, it is idle to attempt to make a final set of grammatical rules which will enable the beginner to translate any and every text which may be set before him. In many sentences containing numerous particles only the general sense of the text or inscription will enable him to make a translation which can be understood. In a plain narrative the verb is commonly a simple matter, but the addition of the particles occasions great difficulty in rendering many passages into a modern tongue, and only long acquaintance with texts will enable the reader to be quite certain of the meaning of the writer at all times. Moreover, allusions to events which took place in ancient times, with the traditions of which the writer was well acquainted, increase the difficulty. This being so it has been thought better to give at the end of the sketch of Egyptian grammar a few connected extracts from texts, with interlinear transliteration and translation, so that the reader may judge for himself of the difficulties which attend the rendering of the Egyptian verb into English.

CHAPTER X.

ADVERBS, PREPOSITIONS, CONJUNCTIONS, PARTICLES.

Adverbs.

In Egyptian the prepositions and certain substantives and adjectives to which ⊂⊃ *er* is prefixed take the place of adverbs; examples are :—

1. The cattle which were before him became

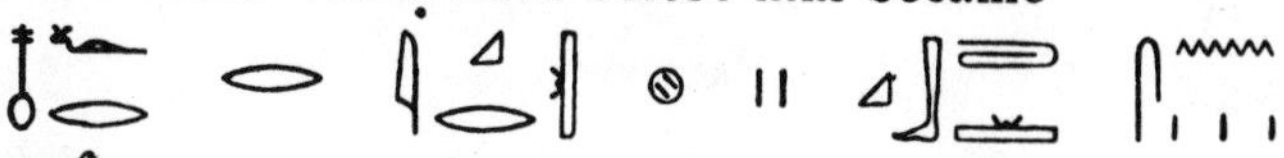

nefer *er* *àqer* *sep sen* *qeb* - *sen*
fine exceedingly, twice, they doubled

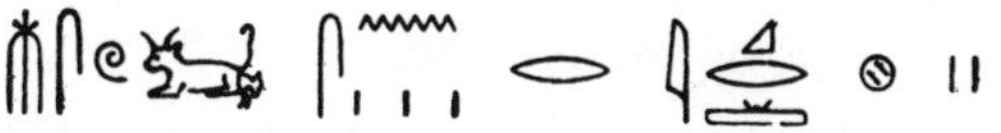

mesu - *sen* *er* *àqer* *sep sen*
their births exceedingly, twice.

2. 

un *set* *nefer* *er* *āa* - *ur* *ḥer* *àb*
Was the woman fair exceedingly to the mind

en *ḥen-f* *er* *χet* *neb*

of his majesty more than any thing.

3. 

åu - f *senṭ* *er* *āa - ur*

Was he afraid exceedingly.

4. 

χāqu - tu *pa* *ḥetrå* *er*

Were cut (wounded) the horses

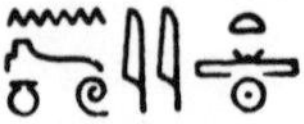

ennuit

immediately.

Prepositions.

Prepositions, which may also be used adverbially, are simple and compound. The simple prepositions are:—

1.  *en* for, to, in, because.
2.  *em* from, out of, in, into, on, among, as, conformably to, with, in the state of, if, when.
3.  *er* to, into, against, by, at, from, until.
4.  or  *ḥer* upon, besides, for, at, on account of.
5.  *ṭep* upon.

6.  *χer* under, with.

7.  *χer* from, under, with, during.

8.  *mā* from, by.

9. 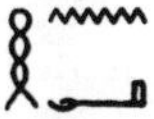 *ḥenā* with.

10.  *χeft* in the face of, before, at the time of.

11. 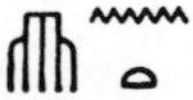 *χent* in front of, at the head of.

12.  *ḥa* behind.

13.  *mȧ* like, as.

14.  *ṭer* since, when, as soon as.

The following are used as prepositions :—

 *ȧmi* dwelling in.

 *ȧri* dwelling at or with.

 *ḥeri* dwelling upon.

 *χeri* dwelling under.

 *ṭepi* dwelling upon.

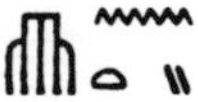 *χenti* occupying a front position.

These are formed from the prepositions  *m*,  *r*,  *ḥer*,  *χer*,  *ṭep*, and  *χent* respectively. The following examples will illustrate the use of prepositions :—

I. 1. 

en *ka* *en* *Ȧusȧr* *ān* *Ani*

To the ka (double) of Osiris, the scribe Ani.

2. 

paut *neteru* *em* *hennu* *en*

The company of the gods [are] in praises because

uben-k

thou risest.

3. 

ta *em* *śertu* *en* *maa* *satet-k*

The earth [is] in rejoicing at the sight of thy beams.

II. 1. 

uben-f *em* *χut* *ȧbtet* *ent* *pet*

He riseth in the horizon eastern of heaven.

2. 

uṭāu *pet* *ta* *em* *māχait*

Weighers of heaven and earth in scales.

3. 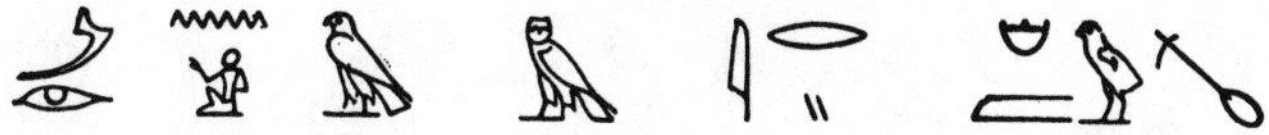

maa - nȧ Ḥeru em ȧri ḥemu

May I see Horus {as the guardian of / i. e., standing at} the rudder.

4. 

qem - f em χet buṭ

May it be found on the wood of the table of offerings.

5. 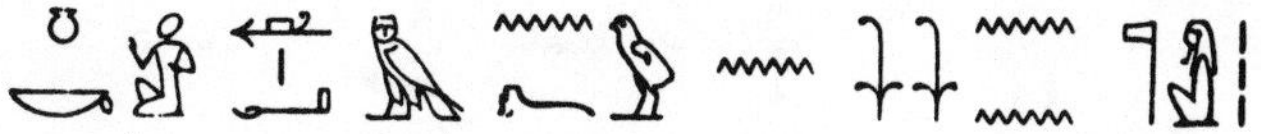

nuk uā em ennu en enen neteru

I [am] one of those gods.

6. 

ȧ uā pesṭ em Āāḥ pert

Hail One shining from the Moon! Cometh forth

Ȧusȧr Ani pen em āšt - k

Osiris Ani this among thy multitude.

7. 

em hamemet un - nȧ

In the state of the *hamemet* beings may I lift up my legs

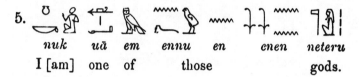

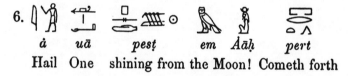

unun Ȧusȧr

[as] doth lift up the legs Osiris.

8. 

àn χenṭ - à ḥer - f em tebt - à

Not let me walk upon it with my sandals.

9. 

em ṭept - re pert em

Conformably to the utterance [which] came forth from

re ḥen en Ḥeru

the mouth of the majesty of Horus.

III. 1. 

àu-f ḥer šemi em - sa naif

He followed after his

àaut er seχet

cattle in the fields.

2. 

er paif per er tennu

Into his house at each

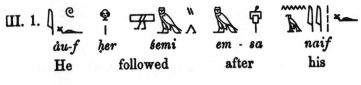

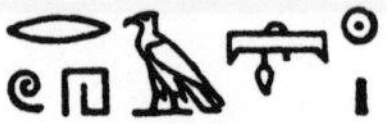

ruha

evening.

3. 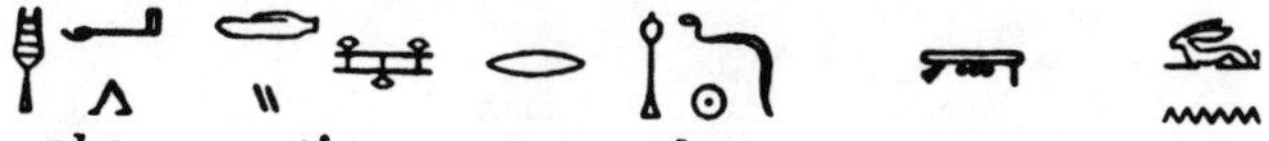

āḥā ṭi er ḥeť - ta un

Stand up, wait until the daybreak being

pa àten ḥer uben

the Disk, *i. e.*, Rā, shining (*or* rising).

4. 

ḥept - tu Maāt er tràui

Embraced art thou by Maāt at the two seasons.

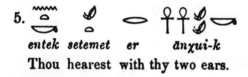

5. 

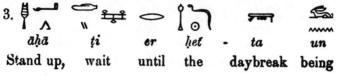

entek setemet er ānχui-k

Thou hearest with thy two ears.

6. 

em āḥā er-à em meter

Let none stand up against me in evidence,

em χesef er-à em ťaťat

none make opposition to me among the chiefs.

7. 

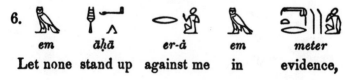

men àb - k er āḥāu - f

Stable is thy heart by (*or* on) its supports.

8. 

seχem - å *em* *utu*

I have gained the mastery of what was commanded

årit *er - å* *ṭep* *ta*

to be done for me upon earth.

IV. 1. 

Teḥuti Maāt ḥer āui - f

Thoth and Maāt upon his two hands (*i. e.*, on the right and left).

2. 

ṭā - k *maa-tu* *ḥer* *ṭep* *ṭuait*

Thou lettest be seen thyself at {the head of the morning, *i. e.*, the early morning,}

hru *neb*

each day.

3. 

āḥā *āḥa - nef* *ḥer - s*

He hath fought for it.

4. 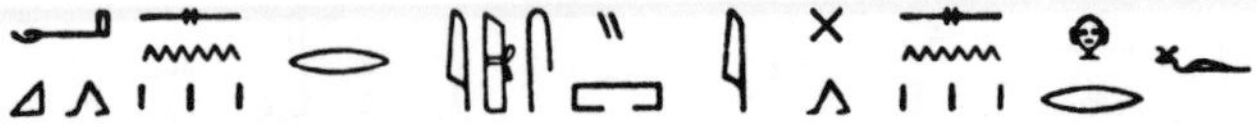

āq - sen *er* *åsi - å* *seś - sen* *ḥer - f*

They enter into my sepulchre, [or] they pass by it.

5. 

i-ȧ nek ȧθi neb-ȧ ḥer

I have come to thee, O Prince, my lord, for the sake

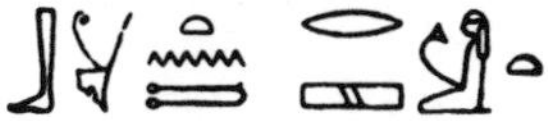

Bent-enθ-reŝt

of Bent-enth-resht.

V. 1. 

ȧr ḳert reχ re pen semaāχeru-

If now be known chapter this he will be made

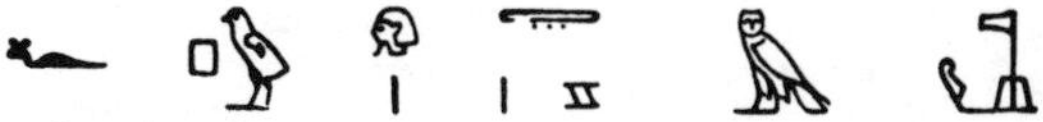

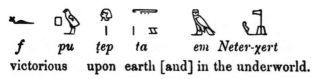

f pu ṭep ta em Neter-χert

victorious upon earth [and] in the underworld.

2. 

maa-ȧ neferu-k uṭa-ȧ ṭep ta

I shall see thy beauties, I shall be strong upon earth.

VI. 1. 

ȧp en pa ser en Beχten iu

An envoy of the Prince of Bekhten hath come

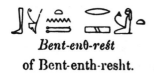

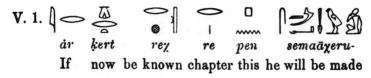

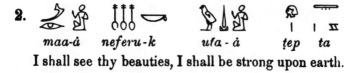

χer ȧnut āŝt en suten ḥemt

with gifts many for the queen.

2. 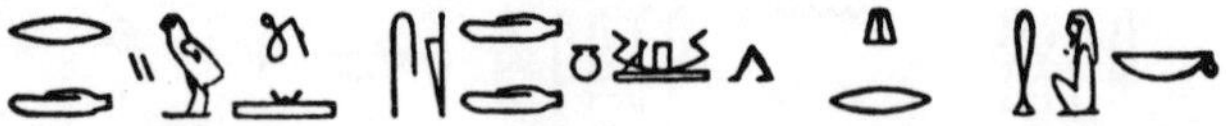

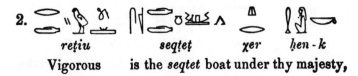

reṭiu *seqṭeṭ* *χer* *ḥen-k*

Vigorous is the *seqtet* boat under thy majesty,

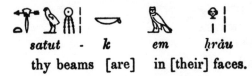

saṭut - *k* *em* *ḥrȧu*

thy beams [are] in [their] faces.

3. 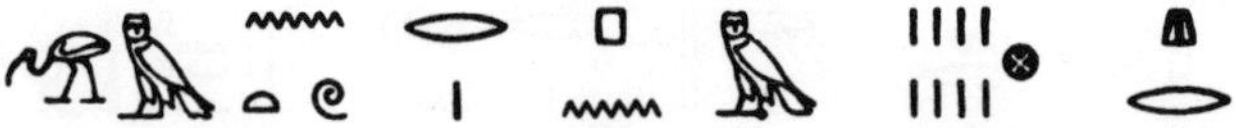

qem-en-tu *re* *pen* *em* *Χemennu* *χer*

Was found chapter this in Hermopolis under

reṭiu *en* *ḥen* *en* *neter* *pen*

the two feet of the majesty of god this.

VII. 1. 

ṭeṭ *ȧn* *suten* *pa* *neter* *āa*

Spake the king, the god great

χer *seru* *ḥāuti*

with the princes [and] chiefs.

2. 

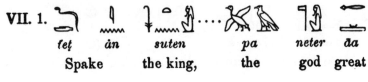

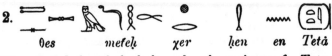

θes *meṭeḥ* *χer* *ḥen* *en* *Tetȧ*

[I was] girded with the belt under the majesty of Teta.

3. 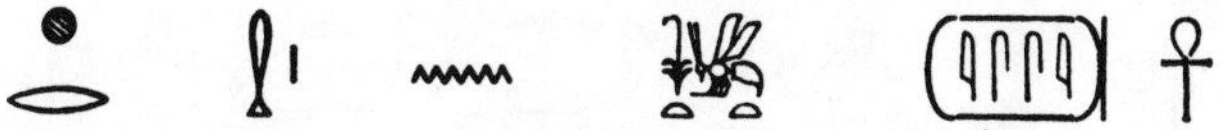

χer ḥen en suten net (or *bȧt*) *Ȧssȧ ānχ*

Under the majesty of {the king of the South and North,} Assa, living

ṭetta er neḥeḥ

for ever [and] ever.

VIII. 1. 

ȧu qemt - s mā ḥent ḥer bennut

It is found by women with emerald ore (?).

IX. 1. 

ȧu-f er ḥems ḥenā taif

He sat with his

ḥemt emtuf surȧ

wife, he drank, etc.

2. 

teben-k pet ḥenā Rā maa-k

Thou goest round heaven with Rā, thou seest

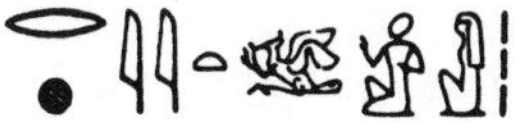

reχit

the beings of knowledge.

3. 

àu sta - tu - f ḥenā suteniu

He is led along with the kings of the south,

neti (or *bàti*) *rā neb*

and the kings of the north each day.

X. 1. 

ṭua Rā χeft uben - f

Praised be Rā when he riseth.

2. 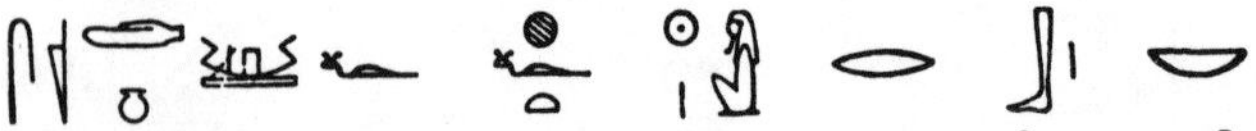

seqṭeṭ - f χeft Rā er bu neb

He journeyeth before Rā into place every

meri - f àm

wisheth he [to be] there.

3. 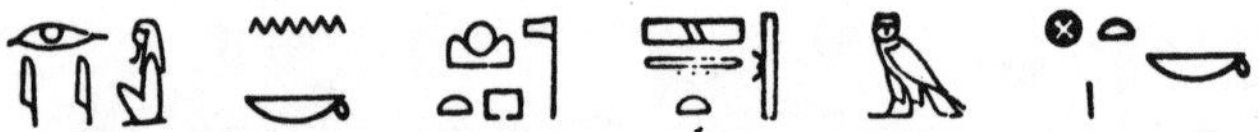

àri-à nek χut šetat em nut - k

I made for thee a hidden horizon in thy city

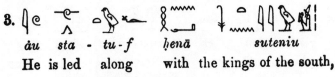

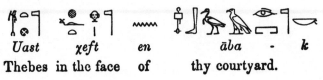

Uast χeft en āba - k

Thebes in the face of thy courtyard.

XI. 1. 

Ȧmen *neb* *nest* *taui* *χent*

Amen, lord of the thrones of the world, at the head

Ȧpt

of the Apts (Karnak).

2. 

VI *pu* *ḳerθ* *ȧm* *χent* *mu*

The sixth who is there is at the head {of the watery abyss.}

XII. 1. 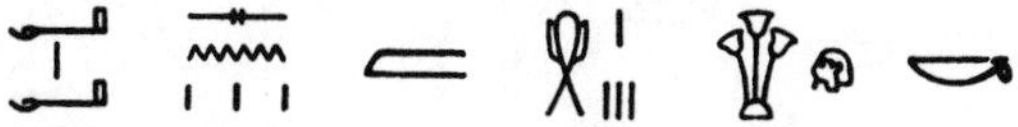

āui - sen *em* *sau* *ḥa - k*

Their hands [are] as protectors behind thee.

2. 

mest *ṭefaut* *en* *neteru*

Producer of the food of the gods

ḥa *karȧ*

behind the shrines.

3. 

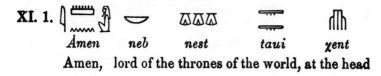

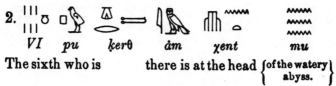

rer - nȧ *ḥa* *suḥt - f*

I go round behind his egg.

XIII. 1. 

ṭā-tu nȧ ḥetepu em baḥ mȧ

May be given to me offerings in the presence as [to]

šesu Ḥeru

the followers of Horus.

2. 

i - kuȧ χer - ten ṭer - ten

I have come before you, do ye away with

ṭu neb ȧri - ȧ mȧ ennu

evil all dwelling in me like that [which]

ȧri en ten en χu VII ȧpu

ye did for spirits seven these

ȧmiu šes en neb - sen

who [are] in the following of their lord

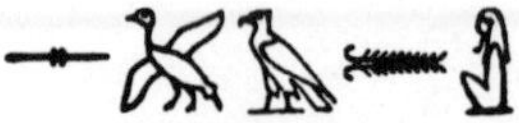

Sepa

Sepa.

XIV. 1. 

su uār er ḥāt ḥen - f ṭer

He fled before his majesty when

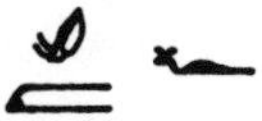

setem - f

he heard [of him].

2. 

ṭeḳa - à nehaut sentrà

I planted sycamores and incense-bearing trees

em paik āba bu

in thy courtyard, never

petrà - u ān ṭer reku neter

were seen [such as] they going back since {the time of the god.}

3. 

àm - à às ta en ḥeqt ses à

I have eaten, behold, bread of sorrow, I have drunk

mu em àb ṭer hru pef

water of affliction since day that

setem-k ren - à

[in which] thou didst hear my name.

Examples of the words which are like prepositions are :—

1. 

ànet ḥrà-k àmi em ḥetepu neb

Homage to thee dweller in peace, lord

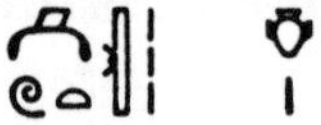

āut àb

of joy of heart!

2. 

χā - θà em neb Ṭāṭāu em ḥeq

Thou art crowned as lord of Tattu, [and] as prince

àmi Àbṭu

dwelling in Abydos.

3. 

sefeχ - nà àsfet àrt - θen

I have set free the faults which dwell in you.

4. 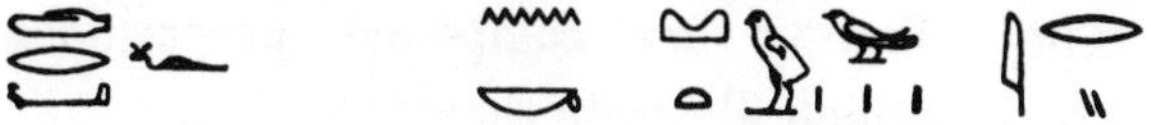

ṭer - f *nek* *ṭut* *ȧri*

He hath done away for thee the evils dwelling

ḥāu - k *em* *χu* *ṭep - re - f*

in thy members by the power of his utterance.

5. 

ȧu-f *ḥer* *ennu* *χeri* *pa* *sba*

He looked under the door

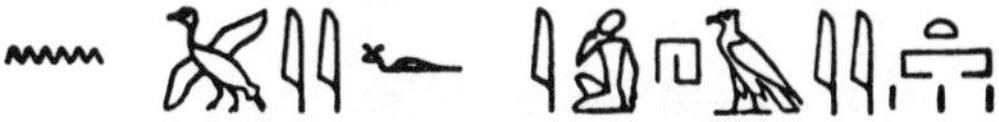

en *paif* *ȧhait*

of his stable.

6. 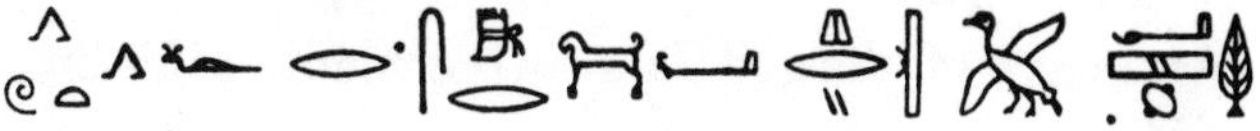

i-tu-f *er* *seṭer* *χeri* *pa* *āś*

He came to lie down under the {cedar tree.}

7. 

nuk *χenti* *Re - stau*

I am at the head of Re-stau.

8. 

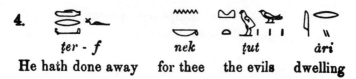

nuk *ka* *em* *χenti* *seχet*

I am the bull at the head of the field.

The following are compound prepositions with examples which illustrate their use.

1.  *em àsu* in consequence of, in recompense for.

ṭā - nef ḥeq-à Qemt Ṭeśert em

He hath granted me to rule Egypt and the desert in

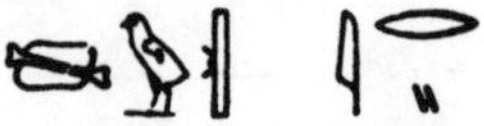

àsu àri

reward therefor.

2. 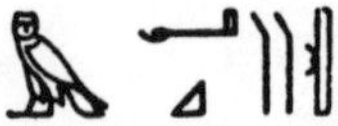 *em āq* in the middle.

tut en Fa-ā em āq ḥāti - f

An image of the god Fa-ā in the middle of his breast.

3. 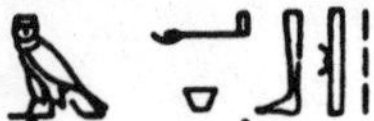 *em āb* or 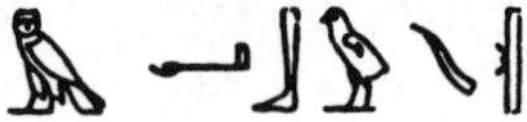 *em ābu* opposite.

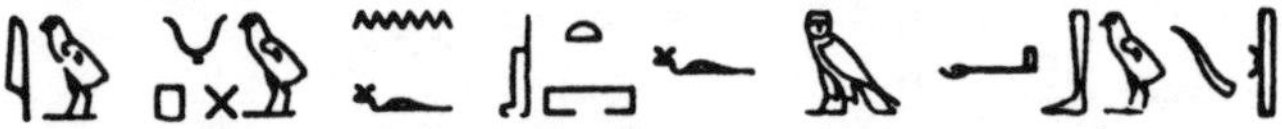

àu àpu - nef àuset-f em ābu

Is ordered for him his seat opposite

sebau

the stars.

4  *em uā* alone.

āḥā ser em uā seṭi ses

Stood the prince alone, he drew the bolt.

5.  *em uaḥ ḥer* in addition to.

ki sa ȧmθ ābu em uaḥ ḥer

Another order among the priests in addition to

sa IV

the orders four [already existing].

6. 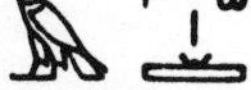 *em baḥ* before, in the presence of.

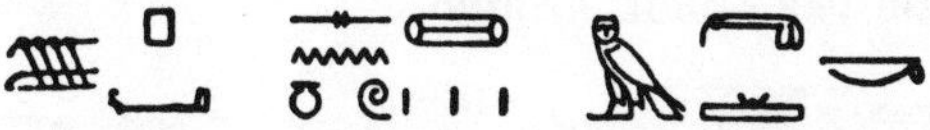

seśep sennu em baḥ - k

The receiving of cakes before thee.

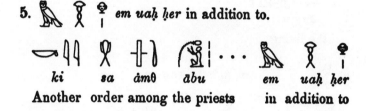

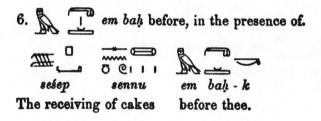

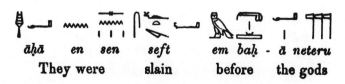

āḥā en sen seft em baḥ - ā neteru

They were slain before the gods

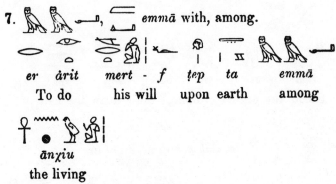

7.  *emmā* with, among.

er *årit* *mert - f* *ṭep* *ta* *emmā*

To do his will upon earth among

ānχiu

the living

8.  *em måtet* likewise.

em *måtet* *emtuk* *i - nek* *er*

Likewise thou come to

seχet *χeri* *pertu*

the fields with grain.

9.  *em rer* about, around.

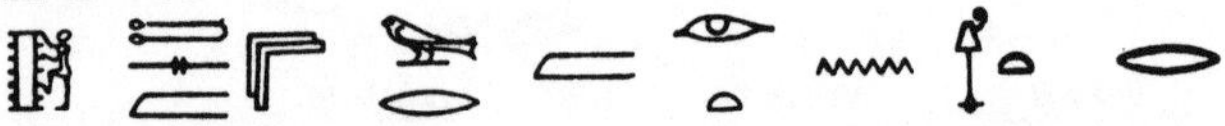

qeṭ *θesem* *ur* *em* *årit* *en ḥemut* *er*

Building a bastion great with work of artificer by the

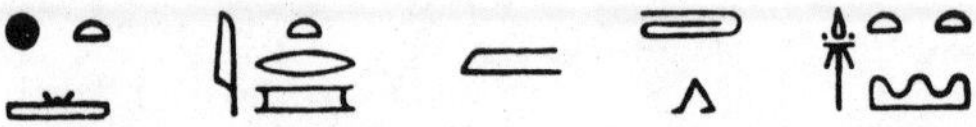

χet *åter* *em* *rer* *åbtet*

work of the river about the eastern side.

10.  *em nem*,  *em nem-ā* a second time, again.

àn *mit* - *nef* *em* *nem*

Not shall he die a second time.

11.  *em ruti* outside.

per - *f* *per-à* *em* *ruti*

He cometh forth, I come forth outside.

12.  *em ḥau* moreover, besides, in addition to.

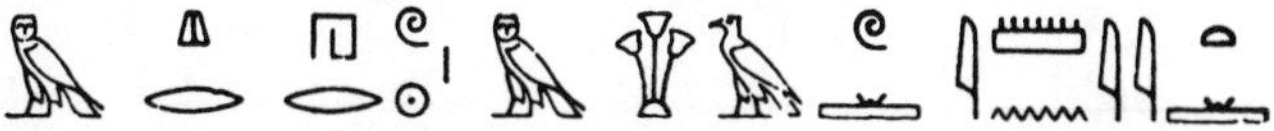

em *χer* *hru* *em* *ḥau* *àmenit*

In the course of the day besides continually.

13.  *em ḥāt* before, in front of.

àb - *k* *neṭem* *ārāti* *χā* - *θ* *em* *ḥāt* - *k*

Thy heart is glad, the uraeus riseth before thee.

14.  *em ḥer* in front of, upon.

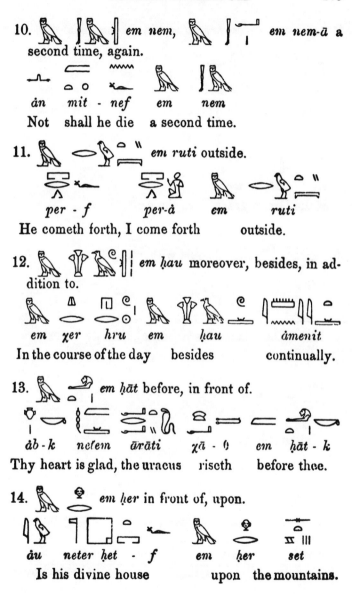

àu *neter* *ḥet* - *f* *em* *ḥer* *set*

Is his divine house upon the mountains.

15.  *em ḥer àb* within, in the midst of.

aà *Nibinaitet* *enti* *em* *ḥer*

The island of Cyprus which [is] in the midst

àb *Uat - ur*

of the Green great (*i. e.*, the sea)

16.  *em χem* without.

uaḥ *ka-f* *àn* *àrit-à* *em*

{He (i. e., God)} hath placed his *ka* [in me], not do I work

χem - f

without him.

17.  *em χennu* within, inside.

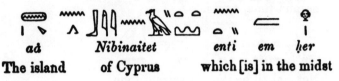

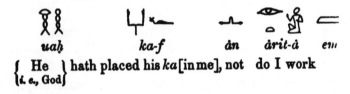

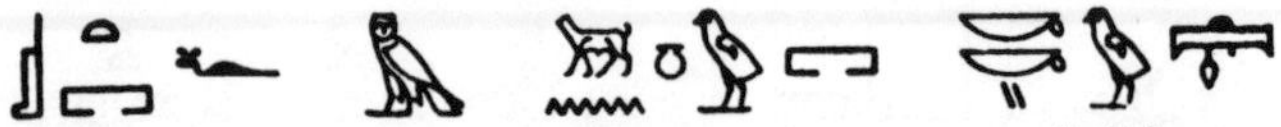

àuset *f* *em* *χennu* *kekiu*

His seat is within the darkness.

18.  *em χer* among.

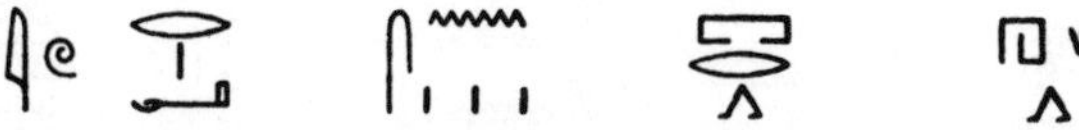

àu erṭā - sen per hi

May it be granted to them to come forth advancing

em χer ḥesu ent Àusàr

among the favoured ones of Osiris.

19.  *em χet* after, behind, in the train of.

àu - f āq - f em χet pert em

He shall enter in after coming forth from

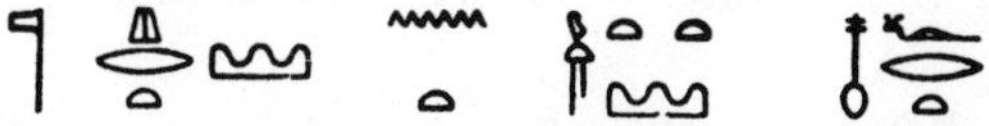

neter χert ent Àmentet nefert

the underworld of Amentet the beautiful.

20.  *em sa* after, behind, at the back of.

sàti Śu iu em sa - k

The slayers of Shu come at thy back

er ḥesq ṭep - k

to cut off thy head.

21. 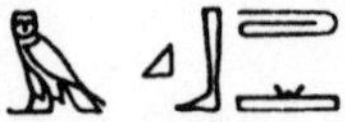 *em qeb* among, in the company of.

un - nȧ em qeb ḥesi emmā

Let me live in the company of the favoured ones among

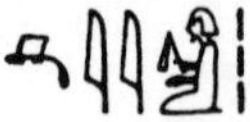

ȧmaχiu

the venerable ones.

22. 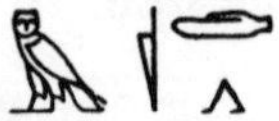 *em qeṭ* around, in the circuit of.

qeṭ - ȧ sebti em qeṭ - s

I built a wall round about it.

unen bes āšt em qeṭet - f neb

There shall be flames many round about it every [where] (*i. e.*, throughout).

23.  *em ṭep* upon.

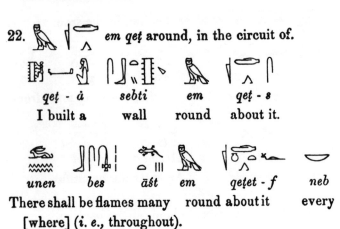

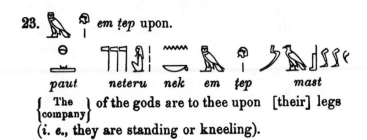

paut neteru nek em ṭep mast

{The company} of the gods are to thee upon [their] legs (*i. e.*, they are standing or kneeling).

24.  *em ṭebu* in return for.

àri - nef màtet emχet menànàu-

{Shall be done} for him the like after his death

f em ṭebu àru àri - nef nà

in return for the things which he hath done for me.

25.  *em ter* because of.

àn reχ - f tai er pa

Not knew he [how] to cross over to

enti paif sen šeràu àm em ter

where [was] his brother younger there because of

na en emseḥu

the crocodiles.

àu-f remi em terti

Was he weeping because of

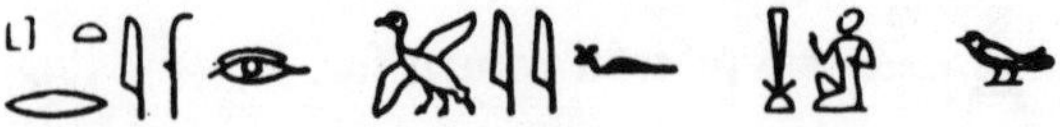

petrȧ *paif* *sen* *šerȧu*

the sight of his brother younger.

26. 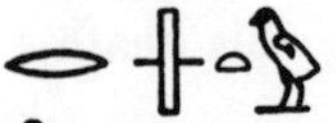 *er ȧmtu* between (also   and ).

teχenui *em* *smu* *benbenet* - *sen*

Two obelisks of *smu* metal their pyramidions

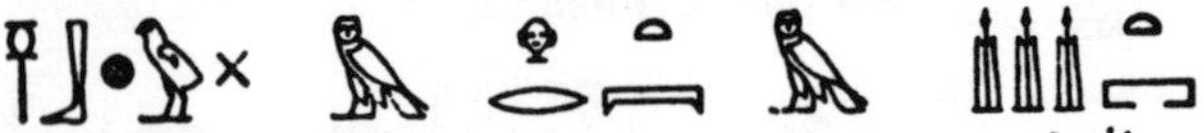

ābχu *em* *ḥert* *em* *ȧnit*

piercing upwards in the colonnade

šepset *er* *ȧmtu* *beχenti* *urti* *en*

noble between the two pylons great of

suten *ka* *neχt*

the king, the bull mighty.

27.  *er ȧuṭ* between.

ȧu *pa* *tut* *en* *pa* *suten*

Was the statue of the king

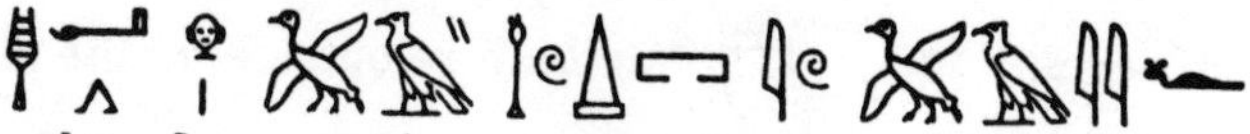

āḥā ḥer pai utu àu paif

standing by the stele was his

Θesemu er àuṭ reṭu - f

greyhound between his legs.

28.  *er āq* opposite.

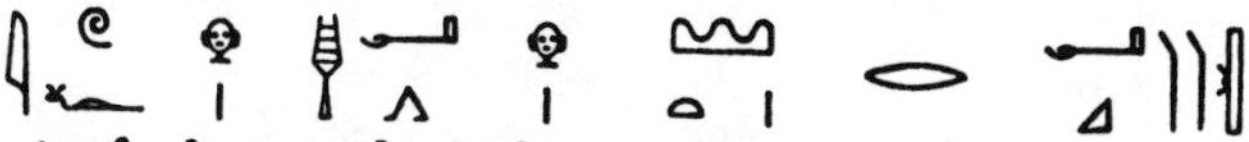

àu-f ḥer āḥā ḥer set er āq

He was standing on the mountain opposite

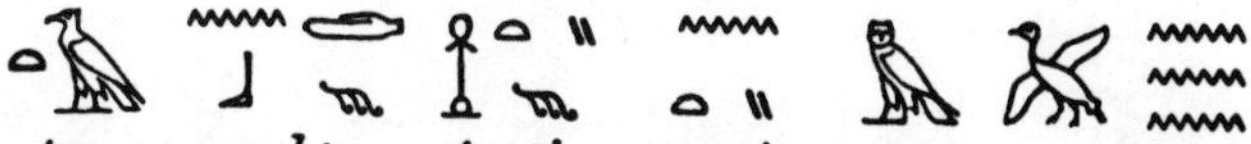

ta nebṭ šenti enti em pa mu

the lock of hair which [was] in the water.

29. 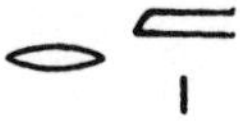 *er ḳes* by the side of.

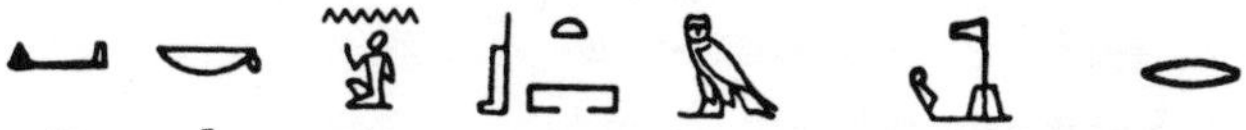

ṭā - k nà àuset em neter-χert er

Grant thou to me a place in the underworld by

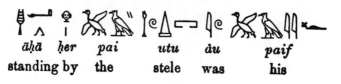

ḳes nebu maāt

the side of the lords of Maāt.

30.  *er bu-n-re* outside, at the place of the door of the way.

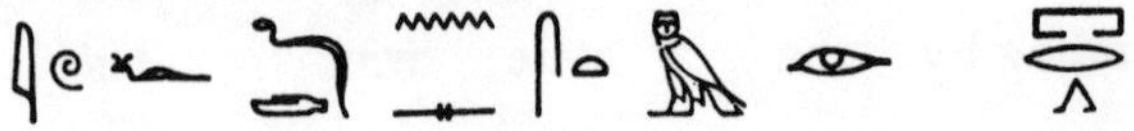

àu-f *ṭeṭ - nes - set* *em* *àri* *per*

He said to her, Do not make an appearance

er *bu - n - re* *tem* *pa*

outside so that not the

imā *ḥer* *àṭa - t*

sea seize thee.

31.  *àrmā* with.

na *māṭaiu* *en* *pa* *χer*

The guards of the cemetery

enti *àrmā - u*

which [were] with them.

32. 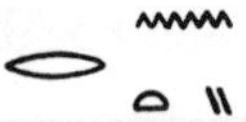 *er enti* because, so that.

er *enti* *betau* *ur* *āa* *pa*

Because an evil very great was that

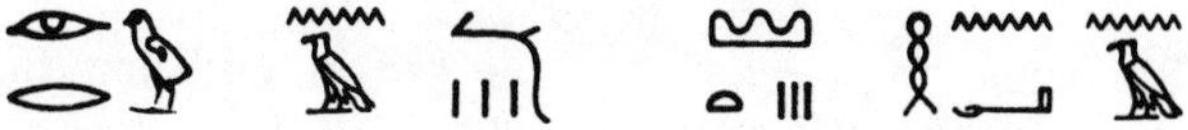

àru na meru set ḥenā na

which had done the governors of the lands towards the

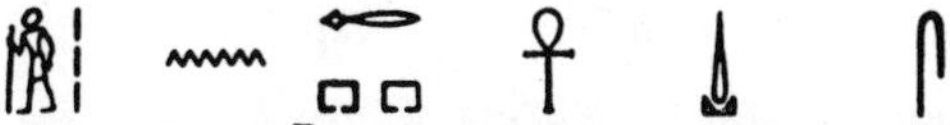

seru en Āa-perti ānχ uta senb

chiefs of Pharaoh, life! strength! health!

33. 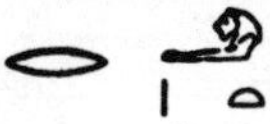 *er ḥāt* before.

emtuf àn naif àaut

He brought his cattle

er ḥāt - f

before him.

34. 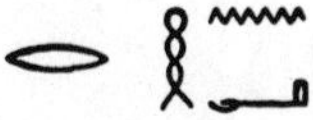 *er ḥenā* with.

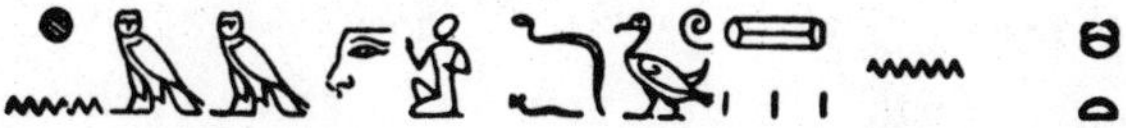

χenemem-à tefau en paut

May I smell the offerings of the company

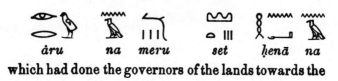

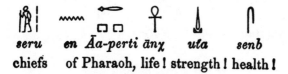

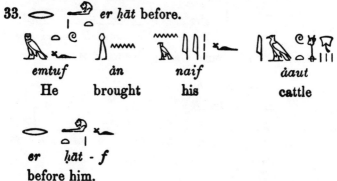

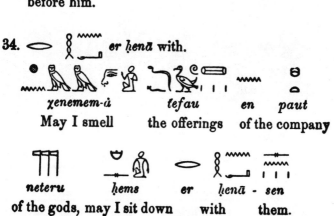

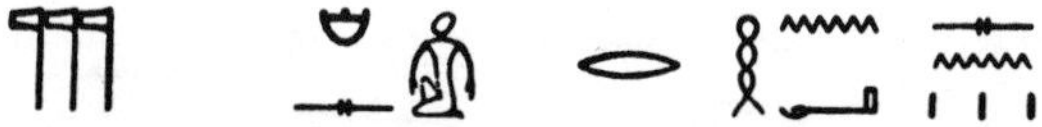

neteru ḥems er ḥenā - sen

of the gods, may I sit down with them.

35. 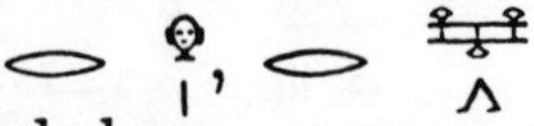 *er ḥer* in addition to, over and above.

er ḥer šetai fetu

In addition to the mysteries recited.

36. 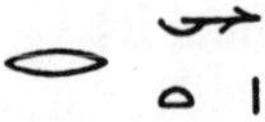 *er χet* after, behind

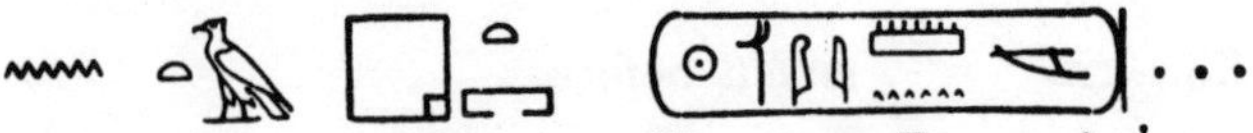

en ta ḥet Usr-maāt-Rā meri Åmen

Of the house of king Usr-maāt-Rā meri Amen

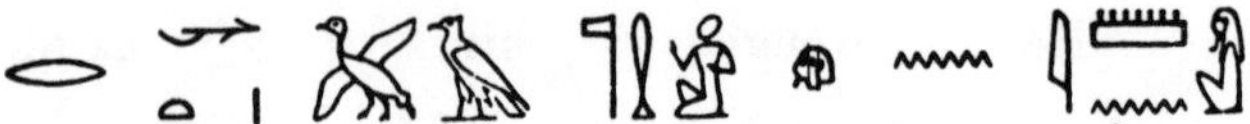

er χet pa neter ḥen ṭep en Åmen

after the prophet chief of Amen.

37. 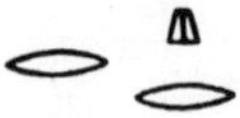 *er χer* with.

perer er χer hau

Coming forth with men and women of the time.

38.  *er šaā* as far as, until.

smen ḥetepet å maāu en ka-å

Establishing my offerings due to my KA,

men *em* *àmenit* *er* *saā*

stablished in perpetuity until

neḥeḥ

eternity.

set *uta* *set* *χui* *māki* *er*

They are safe, they are protected [and] guarded

saā *ḥeḥ*

until eternity.

39.  *er sa* after, at the back of.

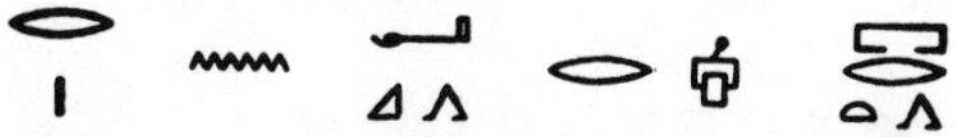

re *en* *āq* *er* *sa* *pert*

Chapter of going in after coming forth.

40.  *ḥer àb* in, within, among, interior.

ḥā *erek* *ḥer àb* *uàa* - *k*

There is rejoicing to thee in thy boat,

qet - k em ḥetepu

thy sailors are content.

em àmentet em àbtet em tauu ḥer àbu

In the west, in the east, in the countries interior.

ànet ḥrà - k Rā neb maāt

Homage to thee, Rā, lord of right,

àmen karà - f neb neteru

hidden is his shrine, lord of the gods,

χeperà ḥeri-àb uaa - f

Khepera in his boat.

41.  *ḥer ā* at once, straightway.

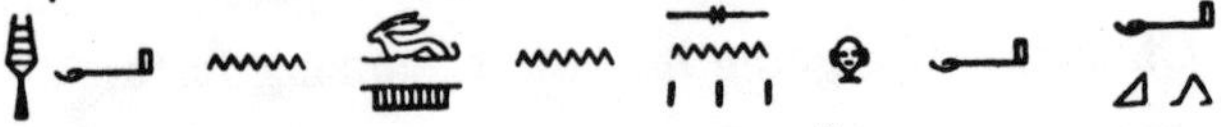

āḥā en un - en - sen ḥer ā āq

They opened the gates at once, entered

en ḥen-f er χennu en nut

his majesty into the city.

42.  *ḥer baḥ* before.

ḥetem *em* *baḥ* *ȧpitu-f* *ḥer* *baḥ*
Destroyed before his judgment [and] before

qennu-f
his punishment.

43.  *ḥer mā* by

ȧri - *en* - *θu* *enen* *ḥer* *mā*
Done was this by

mest *ṭu* *em* *nub* *er* *āu-f*
casing the mountain in gold all of it.

44.  *ḥer χer* beneath.

seqebeb - *ȧ* *ḥer* *χeru* *nehet* - *ȧ*
May I cool myself under my sycamores,

ȧm-ȧ *tau* *en* *ṭāṭā* - *sen*
may I eat cakes of their giving.

45.  *ḥer sa* besides, in addition to, moreover, after.

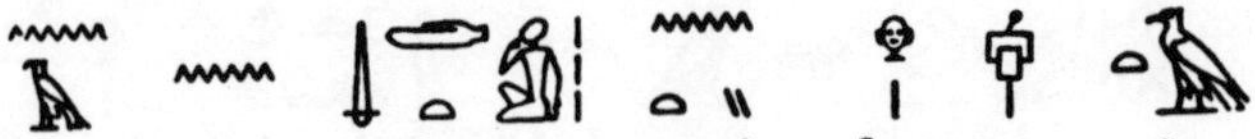

na *en* *meṭet* *enti* *ḥer* *sa* *ta*

The words which are {after *or* in addition to [those of]} the

useχt *maāti*

Hall of Maāti.

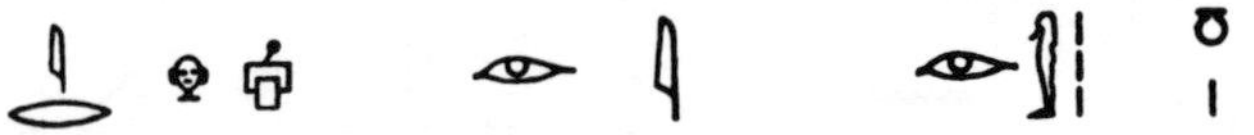

år *ḥer sa* *åri - å* *åru* *nu*

After I had performed the ceremonies of

ṭep renpit ḥeb *uṭen - å* *en* *tef* *Åmen*

{the New-Year festival} I made an offering to father Amen.

46. 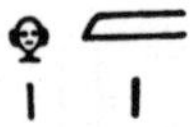 *ḥer ḳes* by the side of.

erṭā - f *meṭet* *ḥer* *ḳes* *åri*

He giveth speech by the side of theirs.

47.  *χer ā* under the hand of, subordinate to.

χer ā - f *er* *ȧnt* *en* *qeres*

Under his hand for the bringing of sarcophagus

pen *em* *Re-au*

this from Re-au (*i. e.*, Mount Ṭura).

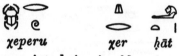

48. 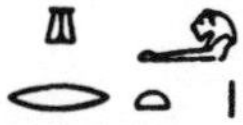 *χer ḥāt* before, in olden time.

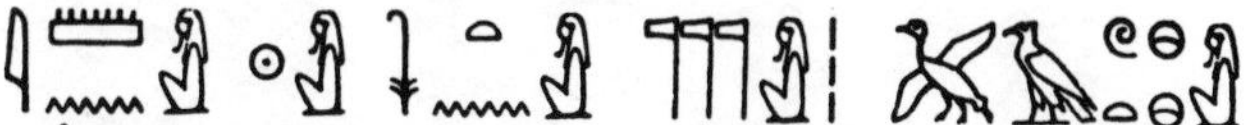

Ȧmen - Rā *suten* *neteru* *pautti*

Amen-Rā, king of the gods {of the two companies[1]}

χeperu *χer* *ḥāt*

[who] came into being in olden time.

49.  *ṭer ā* at once.

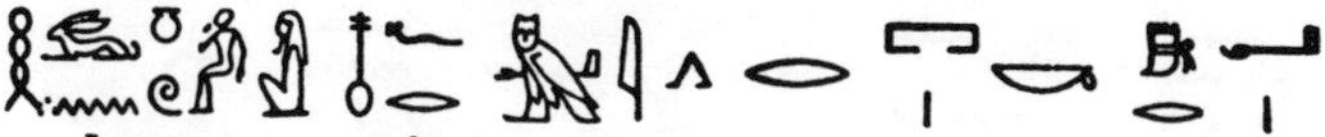

ḥunnu *nefer* *māȧ* *er* *per - k* *ṭer ȧ*

Boy beautiful come to thy house at once!

[1] *I. e.*, 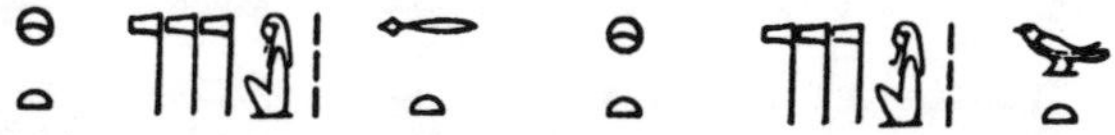

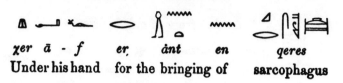

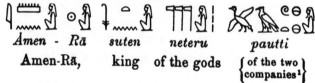

paut *neteru* *āat* *paut* *neteru* *net'eset*

The company of the gods great, the company of the gods little.

50.  *ṭer baḥ* from of old, before.

ȧn sep ȧrit ȧaut ten en

Never was {made (i. e., conferred)} dignity this on

bak neb ṭer baḥ

servant any before.

speru ṭi erek ṭer em baḥ

Coming forth waiting for thee from of old.

51.  *ṭer enti,*  *ṭer entet* because.

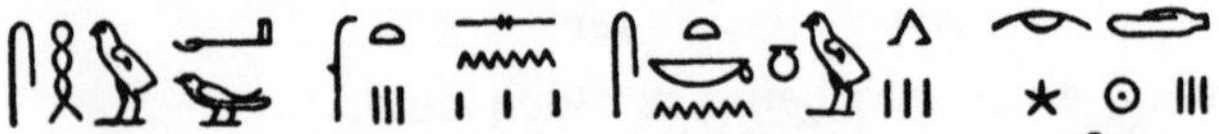

seḥuā renput-sen setekennu ȧbeṭ-

Disturbing their years, they invade their months

sen ṭer enti ȧru en sen ḥet

because they have done evil

ȧmen em ȧrit nek neb

secretly in [their] work against thee all.

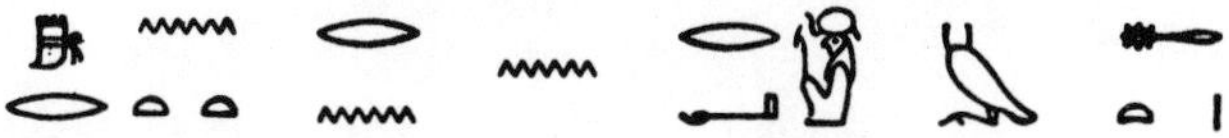

ṭer entet ren en Rā em χat

Because the name of Rā [is] in the body

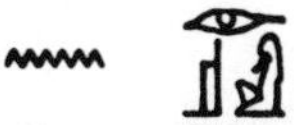

en Ȧusȧr

of Osiris.

ṭer entet-f em uā emmā ennu

Because he is as one among those

ȧu χefti - f ṭer em šenit

whose enemies are destroyed by the divine chiefs.

ṭer entet maa su neteru χu

Because see him the gods, and spirits,

metu em ȧru en

and dead in the forms of

Χenti - Ȧmenti

the Governor of Amentet (*i. e.,* Osiris).

CHAPTER XI.

CONJUNCTIONS AND PARTICLES.

The principal conjunctions are :—

	*en*	because of
	*er*	until
	*ḥer*	because
	*χeft*	when
	*mȧ*	as
	*re pu*	or
	*ȧs*	
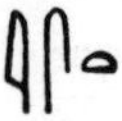	*ȧst*	when
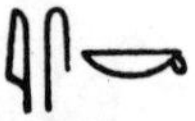	*ȧsk*	
	*χer*	now
	*ȧr*	
	*ȧref*	now, therefore
	*eref*	

PARTICLES.

Interrogative particles are:

 *àn*, which is placed at the beginning of a sentence and is to be rendered by "?"

	*àχ*	what?
	*nimā*	who?
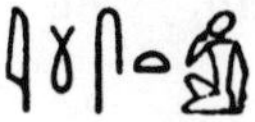	*àqeset*, or *aśeset*, who? what?	
	*tennu*	where?
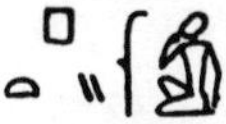	*peti*	what?
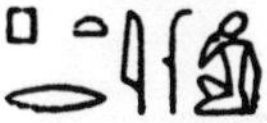	*petrà*	what?

Negative particles are:—

 or 	*àn*	not
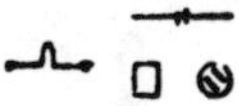	*àn sep*	at no time, never
	*bu*	not
	*ben*	not
	*tem*	not
	*àm*	not.

Examples of the use of these are :—

1. 

neṭer ḥen re pu uā àm-θ ābu

A prophet or one among the priests.

àr reχ śāt (?) ten ḥer ṭep ta àu-f

If be known book this upon earth, he

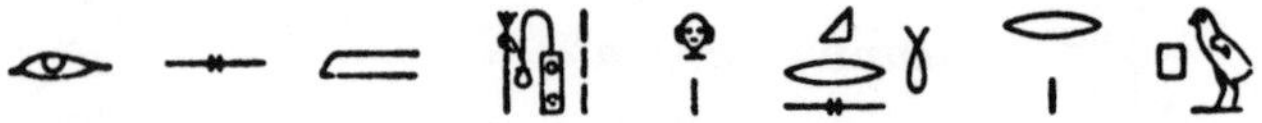

àri - s em ānu ḥer qeres re pu

doeth it in writing upon a bandage or

àu-f per-f em hru neb mer-f

he shall come forth day every he pleaseth.

2. 

às ḥen-f em Neher mà

When his majesty [was] in Mesopotamia according

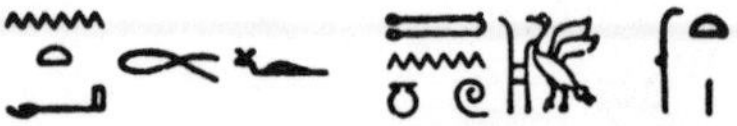

entā-f θennu renpit

to his custom each year.

ȧst ḥen-f ḥer T'ah em utit-f

When his majesty [was] at Tchah in his expedition

sent ent neχt

second of victory.

ȧsk ḥen-f em Uast ḥent

When his majesty [was] in Thebes, the mistress

nut ḥer ȧrit ḥes en tef Ȧmen-Rā

of cities, to do what things pleased father Amen-Rā,

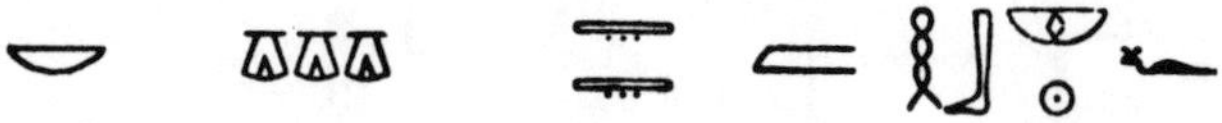

neb nest taui em ḥeb-f

the lord of the thrones of the world, in festival

nefer en ȧp reset

his beautiful of the temple southern.

3. 

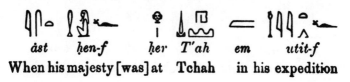

ȧn ȧu ḳer - nek er - s

Shall it be that thou wilt be silent about it?

àn *àu* *àn* *qebḥ* *àb* *en* *ḥen-k*

Is it that not will cool the heart of thy majesty

em *enen* *àri - nek* *sr-à*

at this that thou hast done to me?

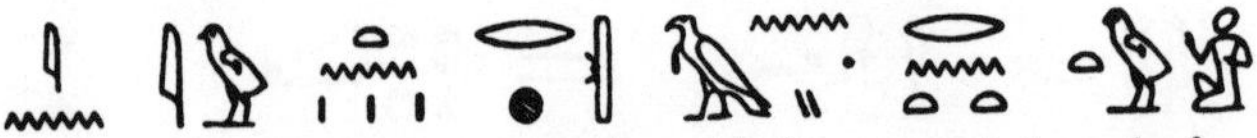

àn *àu - ten* *reχ - tini* *erentet* *tuà*

Is it that ye know not that I even

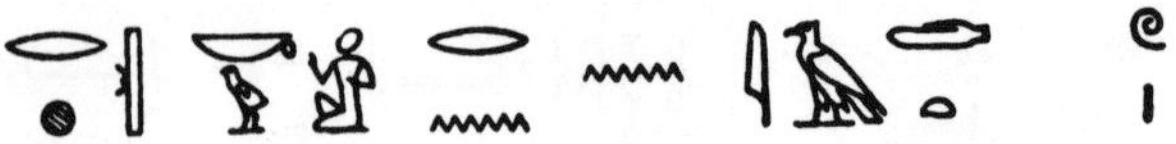

reχ - kuà *ren* *en* *àaṭet*

I know the name of the net?

4. 

teṭ - en - sen *àn* *ḥen-f* *entu-*

Said to them his majesty, "Ye [are]

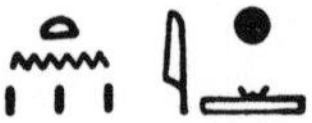

ten *àχ*

what (*or* who)?"

Iḳaṭāi *em* *màtet* *su* *mà* *àχ*

The country of Iḳaṭāi in likeness is it like what?

pa ṭemȧt en χirebu ḥer

The town of Aleppo in

taif mertareȧat pai-

its neighbourhood [and] its

f χet mȧ ȧχ

ford [is] like what?

5. 

un - nȧ nimā trȧ tu entek

Open to me! Who then art thou?

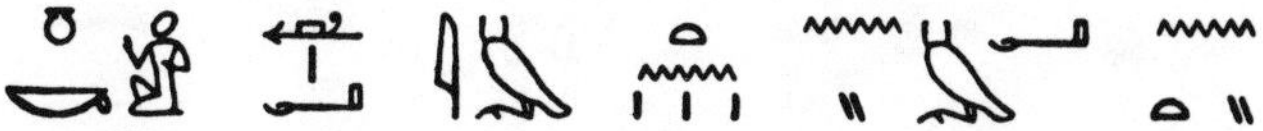

nuk uā ȧm ten nimā enti

I am one of you. Who is

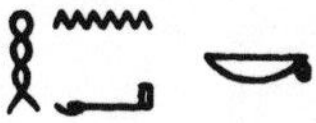

ḥenā - k

with thee?

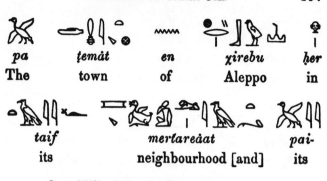

ȧu - set ḥer teṭ - nef ementek en

She said unto him, "Thou art . .

nimā *trȧ*

who then ?"

6. 

ānχ - k *ȧref* *em* *ȧšeset* *χer*

Thou wilt live then on what with

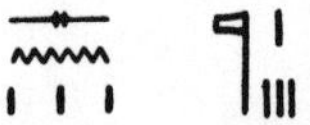

sen *neteru*

them the gods ?

ȧšeset *pu* *χu* *pui* *šem*

What is spirit that [which] goeth

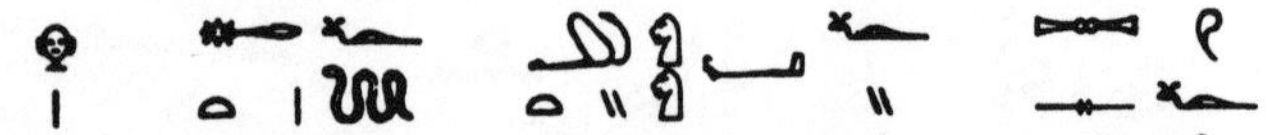

ḥer *χat-f* *peḥti - fi* *θes-f*

upon his belly, [and] his two thighs, [and] his back ?

ȧ *Teḥuti* *ȧšeset* *pu* *χepert* *set* *em*

O Thoth, what háth happened to them,

mesu *Nut*

the children of Nut ?

à *Tem* *àšeset* *pu* *šas - à*

O Temu {what kind of place is this} I have journeyed

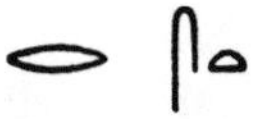

er *set*

into it?

àšeset *pu* *āḥā* *em* *ānχ*

What is [my] duration in life?

(*i. e.*, How long shall I live?)

7.

erṭā *nek* *un - k* *teni*

Shall be given to thee thy food where?

. . . . . . - *sen* *neteru* *er-à*

Say they, the gods, unto me.

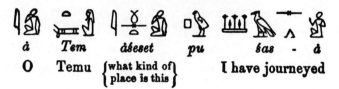

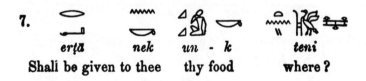

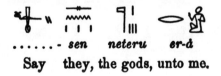

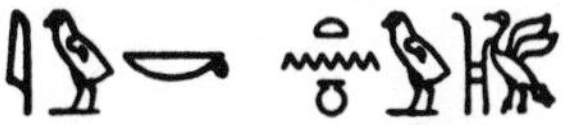

àu-k *tennu*

Thou art where?

8. 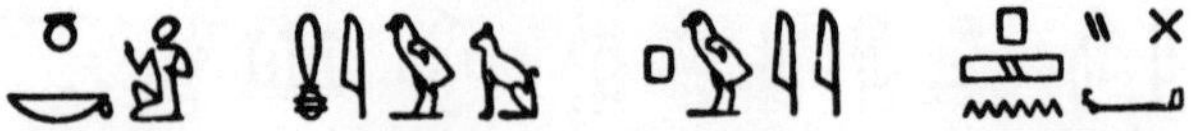

nuk *mȧu* *pui* *pešeni*
I am cat that the fighter (?)

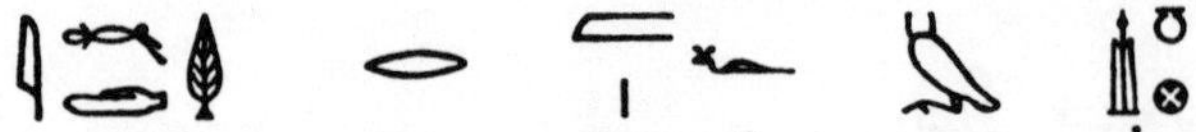

ȧšeṭ *er* *ḳes - f* *em* *Ȧnnu*
of the persea tree by its side in Annu

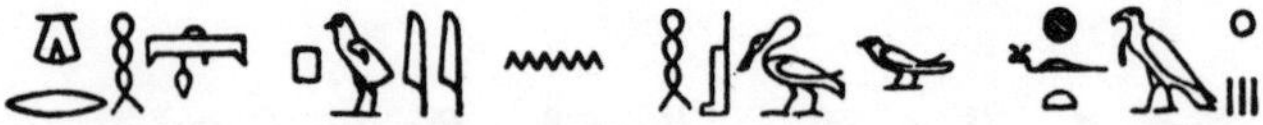

ḳerḥ *pui* *en* *ḥetem* *χefti*
night that of the destruction of the enemies

nu *Neb-er-ṭer* *ȧm-f* *peti* *eref*
of Neb-er-tcher in it. What then is

su *mȧu* *pui* *ṭa* *Rā* *pu* *ṭesef*
it ?[1] Cat that male Rā is himself.[2]

peti *eref* *su* *Ȧn-ȧ-f* *pu*
What then is it ? The god An-ā-f is it
(*i. e.*, it refers to An-ā-f).

[1] *I. e.*, What is the explanation of this passage ?
[2] *I. e.*, That male cat is Rā himself.

petrȧ ren - k ȧn sen er-ȧ

What [is] thy name [say] they to me?

petrȧ maat - nek ȧm

What didst thou see there?

petrȧ ȧn - k en sen ȧu maa-

What didst [say] thou to them? I have seen

nȧ ȧhehii em ennu en taiu

rejoicings in these lands

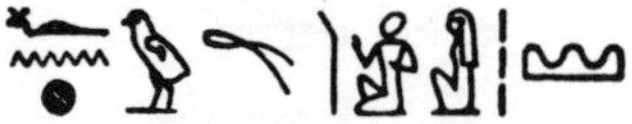

Fenχu

of the Fenkhu.

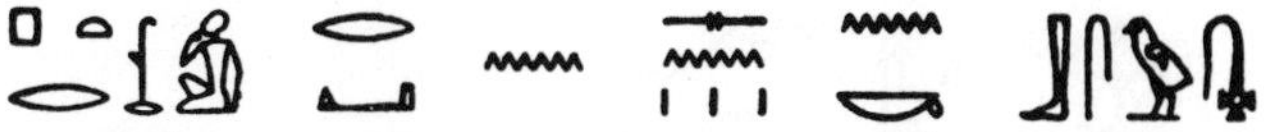

petrȧ erṭā - en - sen nek besu

What did they give thee? A flame

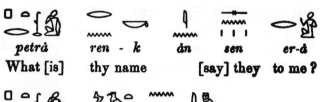

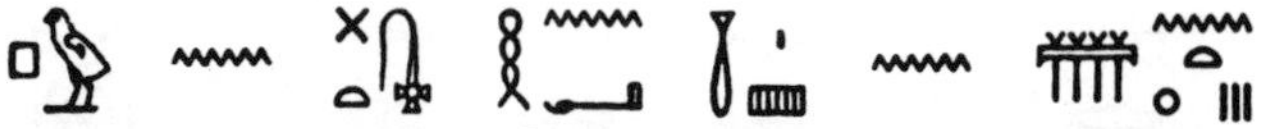

pu en seśet ḥenā uaṫ en θeḥent

of fire, and a tablet of crystal.

petrȧ ȧref ȧrit nek eres ȧu

What then didst thou with it [them]? I

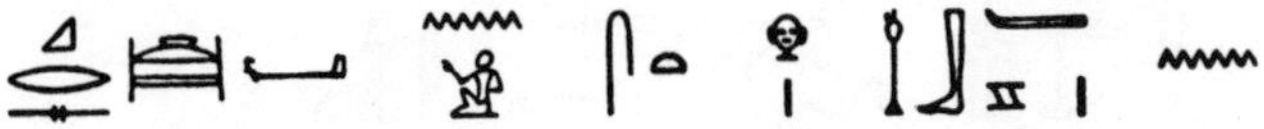

qeres - nȧ set ḥer uteb en

buried them by the furrow of

Māāat em χet χaiu

Māāat as things for the night.

petrȧ qemt - nek ḥer - f uteb

What didst thou find by it, the furrow

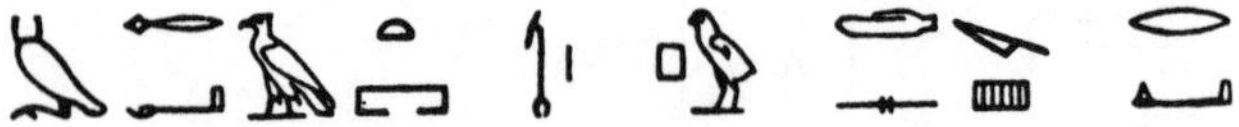

Māat uas pu ṭes erṭā

of Māat? A sceptre flint, 'Giver

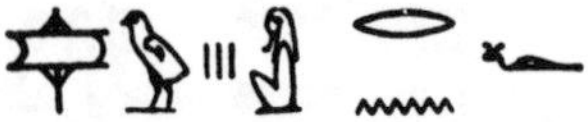

nifu ren - f

of winds' is its name.

petrȧ ȧref ȧrit - nek er pa

What then didst thou with the

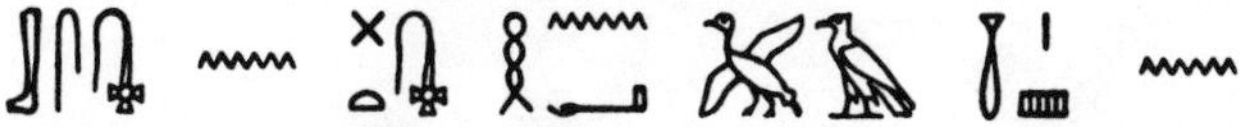

bes en seśet ḥenā pa uat en

flame of fire and the tablet of

θeḥent em - χet qeres - k set

crystal after thou didst bury them?

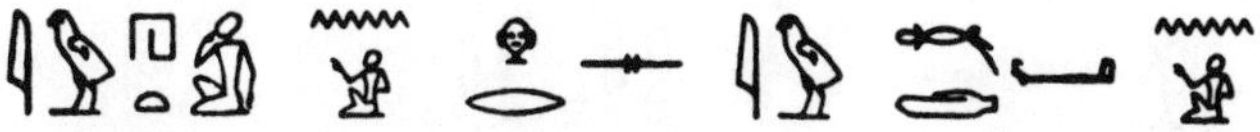

àuhet - nà ḥer - s àu seśeṭ - nà

I said words over them I dug

set àu āχem - nà seśet àu

it up, I extinguished the fire, I

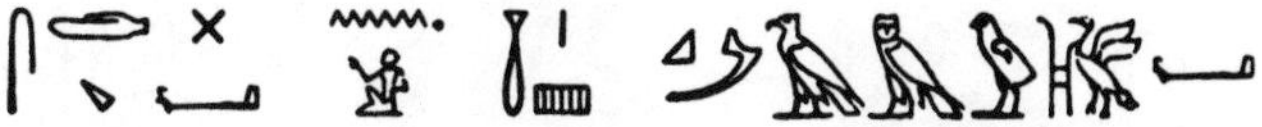

seṭ - nà uat qemamu

broke the tablet, [I] created

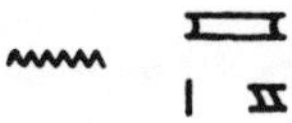

en mer

a pool of water.

9. 

àn χesef - f àn śenā - f ḥer

Not opposed is he, not turned back is he at

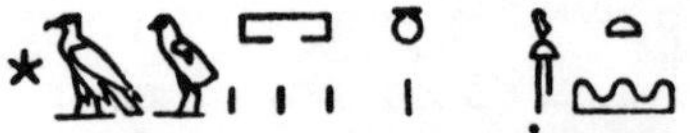

sbau nu Ȧmentet

the doors of the underworld.

ȧn ȧm āut meḥit

Not having eaten goats [or] fish.

ȧn - f su mȧ bȧau en

He brought it as a wonderful thing to

suten χeft maa - f entet seśeta

the king when he saw that [it was] a mystery

pu āa ȧn maa ȧn petrȧ

great, [hitherto] not seen [and] not observed.

ȧn ȧu ḳert ȧn ȧri - entu

For not is it [possible], not can be made

netem-[t]emit ȧm - s

love in it.

10. 

emmā θet - uȧ em ḥaqet

Let me take possession of the captives

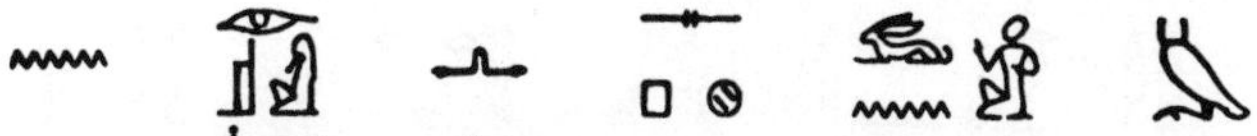

en Ȧusȧr ȧn sep un - ȧ em

. of Osiris, at no time (*i. e.*, never) let me be among

smait Suti

the fiends of Suti.

ȧn sep pat ȧrit mȧtet en

Never before was done the like by

bak neb

servant any.

ȧn sep pa mȧtu setem

Never before the like was heard.

11. 

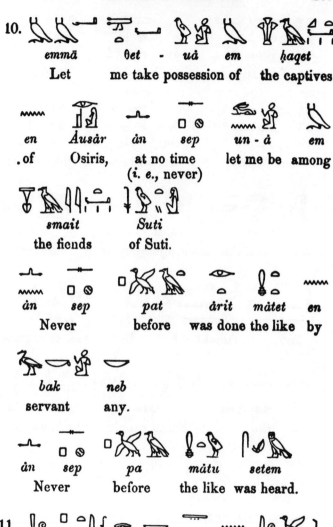

bu petrȧ - k ta en Ȧupa,

Not hast thou seen the land of Aupa? [And]

χaṭumā bu reχ - k qaȧ - f

of Khatumā not knowest thou its form,

Iḳaṭāi em mȧtet su mȧ ȧχ

and Iḳaṭāi in resemblance it [is] like what?[1]

bu ȧru - k utui er Qeṭeś

Not hast thou made a journey to Kadesh

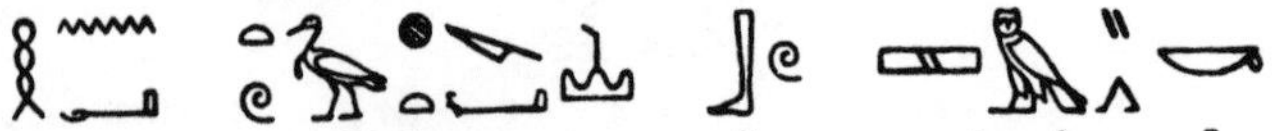

ḥenā Tubaχet bu śemi - k

and Tubakhet? Not hast thou gone

er na en śasu χeri ta

to the Shasu people who have the

pet māśau, bu ṭeḳas - k

bowmen [and] soldiers? Not hast thou passed over

[1] Dost thou not know what kind of place Khaṭumā is, and what sort of land Iḳaṭāi is?

uat *er* *Pamaḳare* *bu* *pui*

the way to Pamakare? Not did

na *àṭau* *reχ* *peḥ - f*

the thieves know [where] he had arrived.

bu *pu* *uā* *ṁeṭet* *mā-à* *ḥeru*

Not [any] one spake with me except

paik *sen* *śeràu*

thy brother younger.

12. 

seχa - sen *ren - à* *ben* *àrit*

May they mention my name, not making

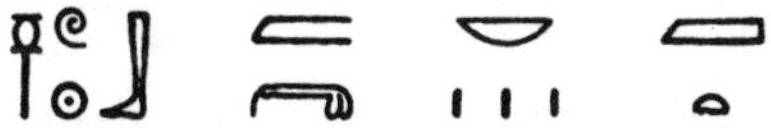

ābu *em baḥ* *nebu* *maāt*

cessation,[1] before the lords of law.

[1] *I. e.*, unceasingly.

às ben àr ém neter - uà

When not I was working

hab - k er àn en - n pertu

thou didst send to bring for us grain,

àu taik ḥemt ḥer feṭ - nà māàì

was thy wife[1] saying to me, 'Come', etc.

13. 

iu-k en - n tem seχau-

Come thou to us not [having] thy memories

k iu-k em àru - k

of evil, come thou in thy form.

tem χesef su em at - f

Not repelling him in his moment.

[1] *I e.,* Was it not when I was working that thou didst send me to fetch grain, [and as I was fetching it] thy wife said to me, 'Come'.

petrȧ set tem - k ṭeṭ

On seeing it do not thou say,

χenś - k ren - ȧ en

'Thou hast made to stink my name before

kaui ḥrȧ nebt

men and women [and] every-body.'

14. 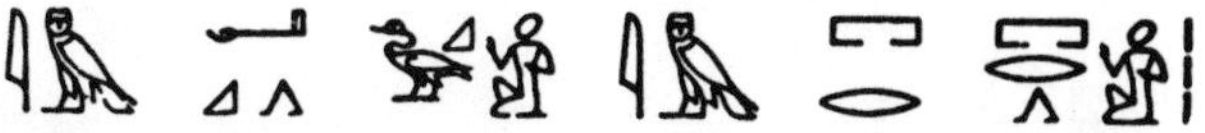

ȧm āq āq ȧm per peru

Not entered a comer in, not came out a comer out,

ȧri ḥen-f merer-f

did his majesty his will.

āḥā en hab - nef en sen em ṭeṭ

He sent to them, saying,

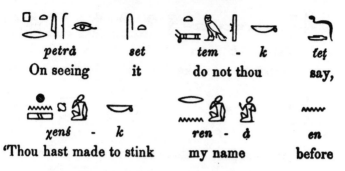

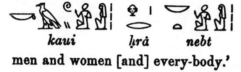

ȧm χetem ȧm āba

Do not shut [your gates], do not fight.

àm - k àri ḥer em reθ

Do not make terror in men and women.

àm - f sàu erek er

Let it not [be] that thou criest out against

setemet-k àm pu en àb

what thou hearest, that there may not be a heart

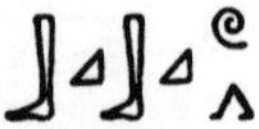

beqbequ

of cowardice (?).

àm-à ah-à en àu

Not shall I suffer I overthrow

nest-à àmt uàa en Rā

from my throne in the boat of Ra

āa

the mighty one.

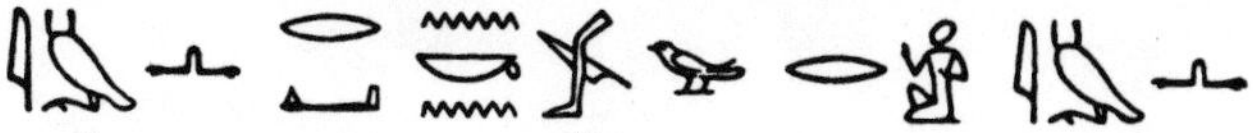

ȧm erṭā neken er - ȧ ȧm-

Do not cause injury to me. Do not

k erṭā ṭep - ȧ ermen ȧm - ȧ

thou cause my head to fall away from me.

ȧm - k ȧri ḥer ḥrȧ nebt ȧpu ḥer

Do not thou perform [it] before people, but only

ḥāu - k ṭes-k

thine own self.

EXTRACTS FOR READING.

I. From an inscription of Pepi I.

[VIth dynasty.] .

111. 

ha *Pepi* *pu* *år* *seθes* - *θu*

Hail Pepi this! Rise up thou,

112. 

āḥā *uāb* - *k* *uāb*

stand up! Pure art thou, pure is

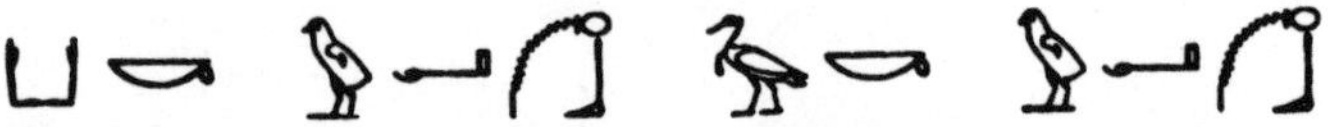

ka - *k* *uāb* *ba-k* *uāb*

thy double, pure is thy soul. pure is

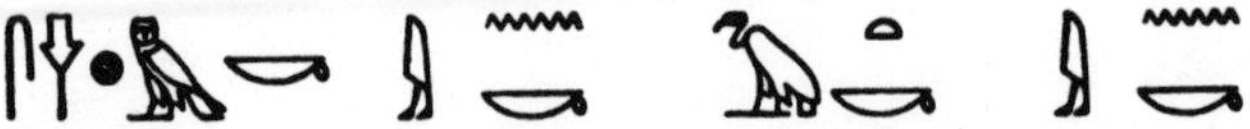

seχem - *k* *i* - *nek* *mut-k* *i* - *nek*

thy power. Cometh to thee thy mother, cometh to thee

Nut *šenem* *urt* *s - uāb - s* *θu* *Pepi*

Nut, the fashioner great, she purifieth thee, O Pepi

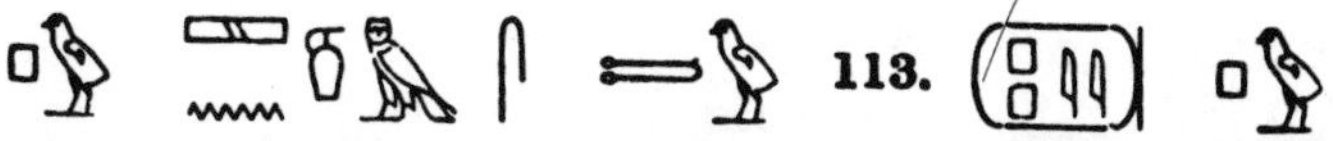

113.

pu *šenem - s* *θu* *Pepi* *pu*

this, she fashioneth thee Pepi this,

χu *ȧs* *ku-k* *ha* *Pepi* *pu*

protecting when thou movest. Hail Pepi this,

uāb - t *uāb* *ka - k* *uāb*

pure art thou, pure is thy double, pure is

seχem - k *ȧm* *χu* *uāb*

thy power among the spirits, pure is

114.

ba-k *ȧm* *neteru* *ha* *Pepi* *pu*

thy soul among the gods. Hail Pepi this,

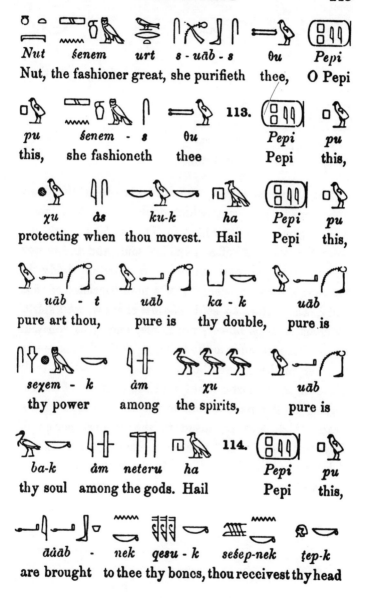

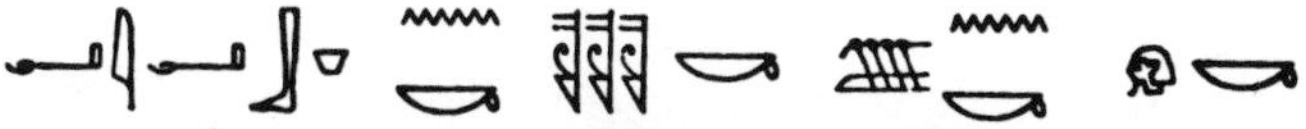

āȧāb - nek *qesu - k* *sešep-nek* *ṭep-k*

are brought to thee thy bones, thou receivest thy head

χer Seb ȧṭer-f ṭut ȧrt-k
before Seb; he destroyed the evil belonging to thee

Pepi pu χer Tem
Pepi this before Tem.

The above passage is an address made to the dead king Pepi by the priest which declares that he is ceremonially pure and fit for heaven. The *ka, ba* and *sekhem,* were the "double" of a man, his soul, and the power which animated and moved the spiritual body in heaven; the entire economy of a man consisted of *khat* body, *ka* double, *ba* soul, *khaibit* shadow, *khu* spirit, *ȧb* heart, *sekhem* power, *ren* name, and *sāḥu* spiritual body. The reference to the bringing of the bones seems to refer to the dismemberment of bodies which took place in pre-dynastic times, and the mention of the receiving of the head refers to the decapitation of the dead which was practised in the earliest period of Egyptian history. Nut was the mother of the gods and Seb was her husband; Tem or Temu was the setting sun, and, in funeral texts, a god of the dead.

II. Funeral Stele of Paneḥesi.

(Brugsch, *Monuments de l'Égypte*, Plate 3.)
[XIXth dynasty.]

1. 

ṭuau *Rā* *χeft* *ḥetep-f* *em*
Adoreth Rā when he setteth on

χut *àmentet* *ent* *pet* *àn* *uā* *àqer*
the horizon western of heaven the one perfect,

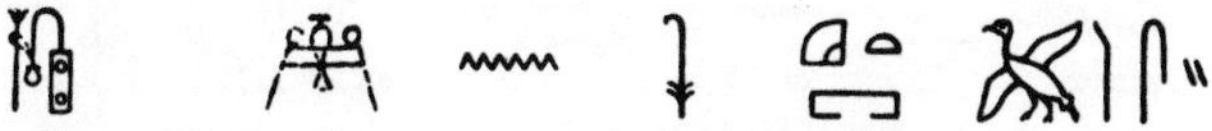

ān *utḥu* *en* *suten* *àpt* *Pa-neḥesi*
the scribe of {the table of offerings} of the royal house, Pa-neḥesi,

ṭeṭ - f *ànet' - ḥrà-k* *Rā* *àri*
[and] he saith :— Homage to thee, O Rā, maker

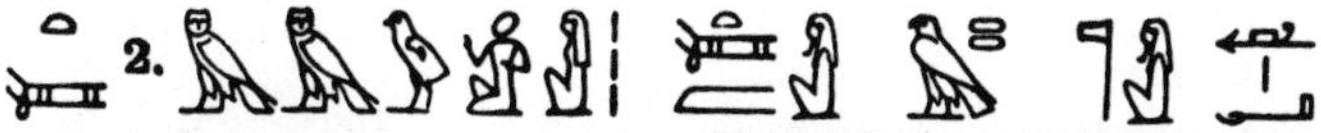

tememu *Tem Ḥeru-χuti neter* *uā*
of mortals, Temu-Harmachis, god one,

ānχ *em* *maāt* *àri* *enti*

living upon right and truth, maker of things that are,

3.

qemam *unenet* *en* *āiu*

creator of {things which shall be,} [and] of animals,

reθ *pert* *em* *maat-f* *neb*

[and] of {men and women,} who come forth from his eye. Lord

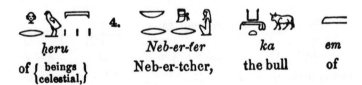

pet *neb* *ta* *àri* *χeru*

of heaven, lord of earth, maker of beings terrestrial [and]

4.

ḥeru *Neb-er-ṭer* *ka* *em*

of {beings celestial,} Neb-er-tcher, the bull of

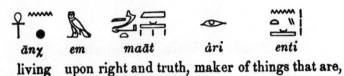

paut neteru *suten* *ḥert* *neb* *neteru*

{the company of the gods,} king of heaven, lord of the gods,

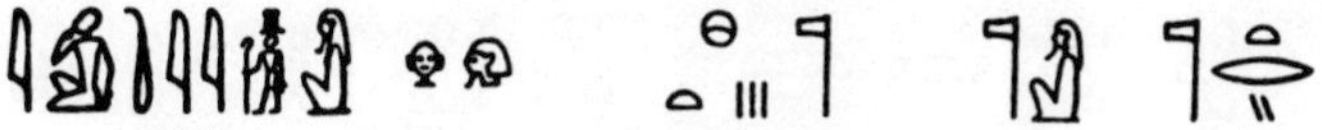

àθi *ḥer* *paut neteru* *neter* *netri*

prince, chief of {the company of the gods,} god divine

5.

χeper *ṭesef* *pauti*

self-created, god of the two companies of the gods

χeper *em* *ḥāt* *hennu* - *nek*

coming into being in the beginning. Praises are to thee,

àri *neteru* *Tem* *seχeper* *reχit*

O {maker of the gods,} Temu making to exist mankind,

neb *benerȧt* *āa* *mert*

lord of sweetness, great of love;

pesṭ - *f* *ānχ* *ḥrȧ* *nebt* *ṭā-ȧ* *nek*

he shineth [and] live mankind. I give to thee

7.

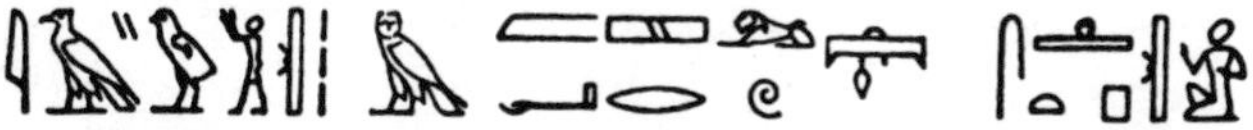

ȧaiu *em* *māśer* *seḥetep-ȧ*

praises at eventide, I make thee to set

tu *ḥetep-k* *em* *ānχ* *åu* *sektet*

[when] thou settest in life. The *sektet* boat

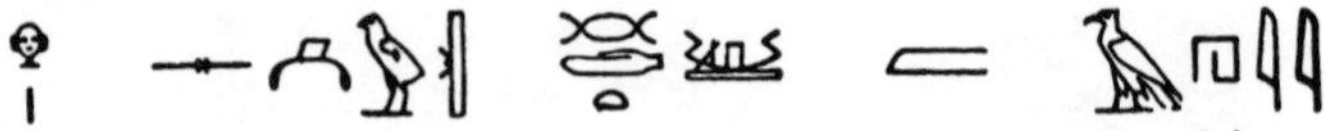

ḥer *seau* *āṭet* *em* *ahi*

is glad, the *āṭet* boat is in joyful

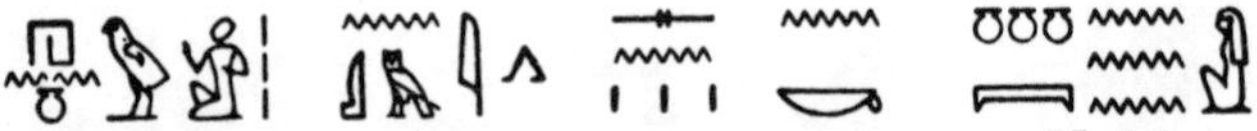

hennu *nemå* - *sen* *nek* *Nu*[*t*]

praising [as] they journey to thee. The goddess Nut

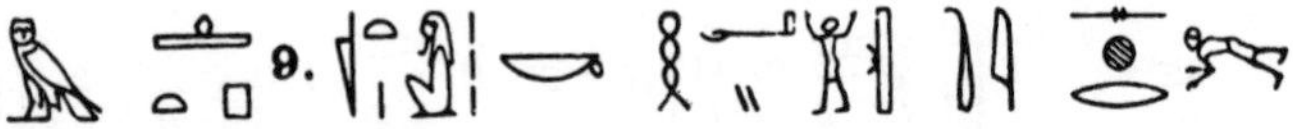

em *ḥetep* *qet* - *k* *ḥāā* - *θå* *seχer*

is at peace, thy sailors are rejoicing; hath over-

en *χut* - *k* *χefti* - *k*

thrown thine eye thine enemy.

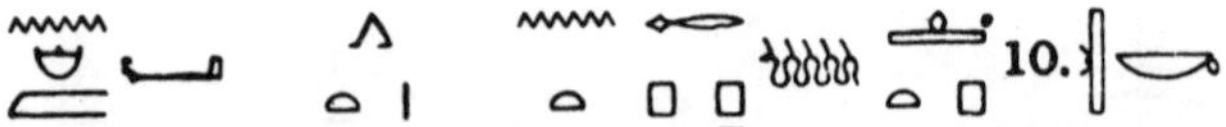

neḥem *reṭ* *ent* *Āpep* *ḥetep* - *k*

Carried away are the leg[s] of Āpep. Thou settest,

nefer *åb* - *k* *au* *em* *χut* *ent* *Manu.*

glad is thy heart joyful in the horizon of Manu.

seḥeṭ - k àm en neter nefer neb

Thou makest light there, god beautiful, lord

ḥeḥ ḥeq Àuḳert ṭā - k

of eternity, prince of Auḳert. Thou givest

seśep en enti àm χefti

thy radiance upon those there, [thy] enemies

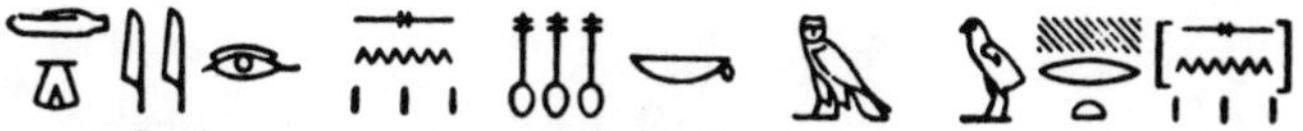

ṭeḳai - sen neferu-k em ...... sen

see thy beauties in their [abodes and]

em tepḥetu - sen āui - sen em

in their habitations [and] their hands

àaui en ka - k àmentiu em

adore thy double; the beings in Amenti

ḥāātu emχet eref pesṭ-k

rejoice after thou hast shone

en sen nebu ṭuat åbu - sen

upon them, the lords of the underworld their hearts

neṭem seḥet - k Åmentet maat - sen

are glad [when] thou lightest up Amentet. Their eyes

14.

sešu en maa - k χentes

open widely at the sight of thee, refreshed

åbu - sen maa - sen tu ḥāā

are their hearts [when] they see thee; rejoiceth

15.

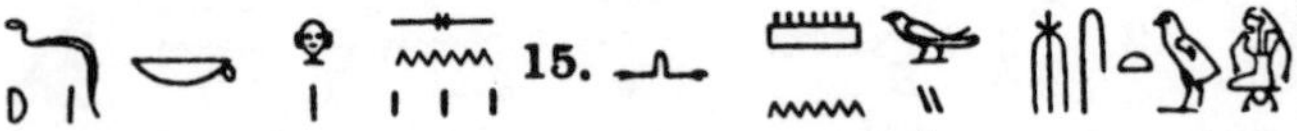

ṭet - k ḥer sen ån meni mestu

thy body through them. Without pain [are] the births

neteṛ ḥāu - sen entek meses-

of god [which are] their members; thou givest birth

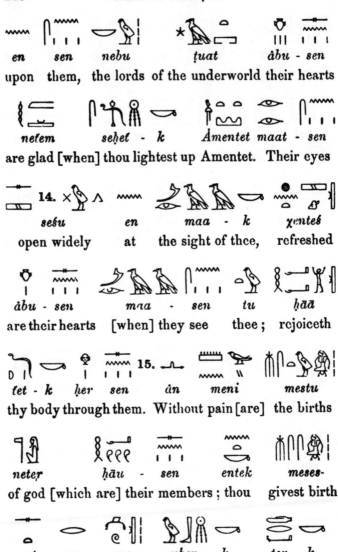

set er au uben - k ṭer - k

to them, all of them. Thou risest, thou destroyest

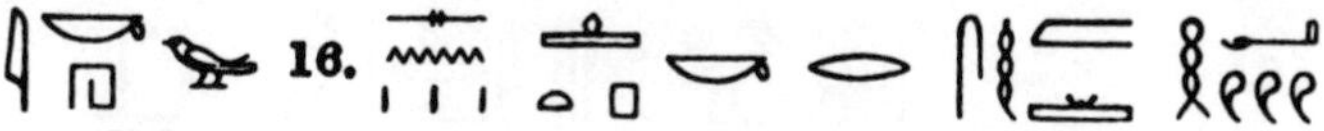

åkeh - sen ḥetep - k er senetem ḥāu-

their grief; thou settest to make glad their

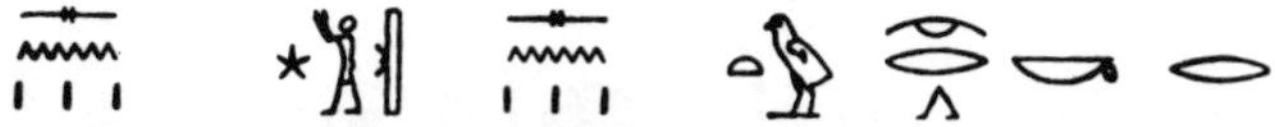

sen ṭua - sen tu sper - k er

members; they praise thee [when] thou comest forth to

sen seśep - sen ḥāt ent uåa-

them, they grasp the bow of thy boat.

k ḥetep - k em χut ent Manu

Thou settest in the horizon of Manu,

nefer - tu em Rā hru neb ṭā - k

happy art thou as Rā day every. Grant thou

un ba - å χenti - sen pesṭ

that may be my soul along with them, may shine

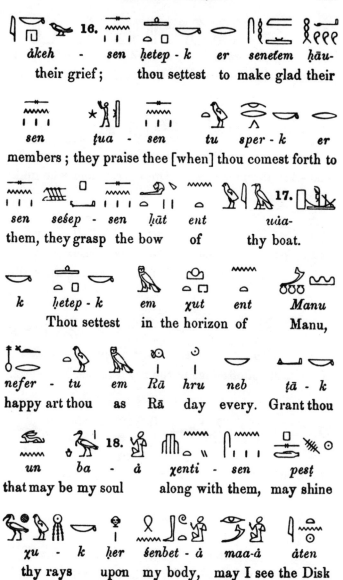

χu - k ḥer śenbet - å maa-å åten

thy rays upon my body, may I see the Disk

19. 

χeft enen χu åqeru nu neter-χert

[being] opposite to those spirits perfect of the underworld

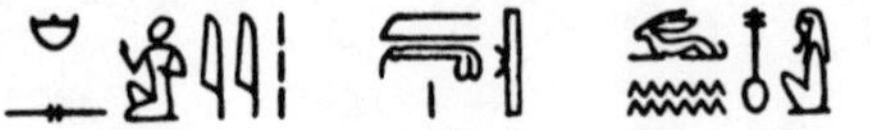 20. 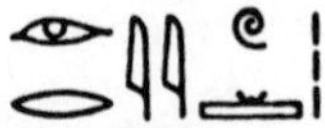

ḥemsiu embaḥ Un-nefer åriu

who sit in the presence of Un-nefer, and who make

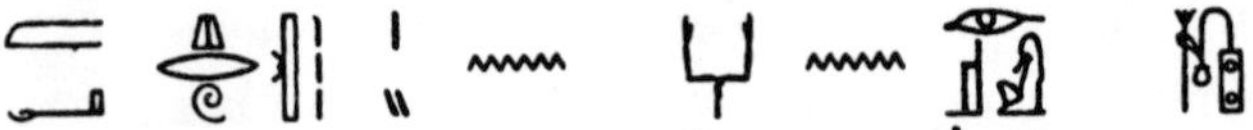

mā χeru en ka en Åusår ān

. . . . . . to the double of Osiris, the scribe

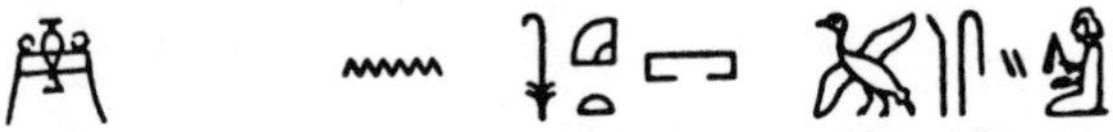

utḥu en suten åpt Pa-neḥesi

of the table of offerings of the royal house, Pa-neḥesi.

21. 

ån sa - f seānχ ren - f

[Dedicated] by his son, who maketh to live his name,

ān netert ent neb taui

the scribe of the goddess (?) of the lord of the two lands,

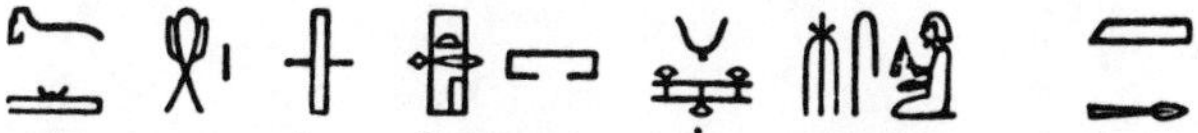

setep sa àm ḥet āat Àp-uat-mes maā-χeru

{worker of magic[1]} in the palace, Ap-uat-mes right of speech (*or* triumphant).

III. Inscription of Ȧnebni.

(Sharpe, *Egyptian Inscriptions*, Plate 56.)

[XVIIIth dynasty.]

1\. 

àrit em ḥeset netert nefert nebt

Made by the favour of the goddess beautiful, lady

taui Rā-maāt-ka ānχ-θ ṭeṭ-θ Rā

of the two lands, Ḥātshepset living, established Rā

mà fetta ḥenā sen - s nefer neb

like for ever, and her brother beautiful, the lord,

àri χet Men-χeper-Rā ṭā ānχ Rā mà

maker of things, Thothmes III., giver of life Rā like

[1] Literally, "protecting by means of the [sign]" which was an object used in performing magical ceremonies.

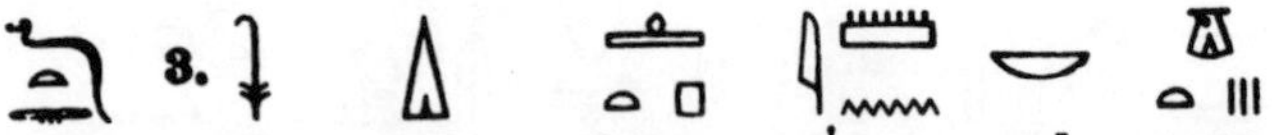

tetta suten ṭā ḥetep Ȧmen neb nest

for ever. King give an offering! Amen, lord {of the thrones}

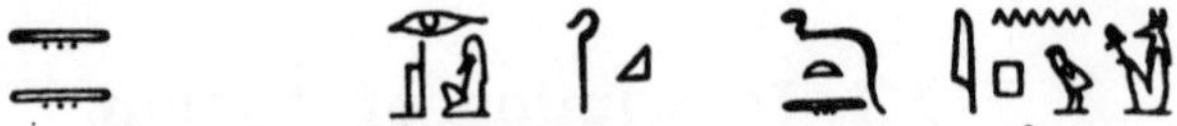

taui Ȧusȧr ḥeq tetta Ȧnpu

of the two lands, [and] Osiris, prince of eternity, Anubis

χent neter ḥet ȧm Ut neb

dweller by the divine coffin, dweller in {the city of embalmment,} lord

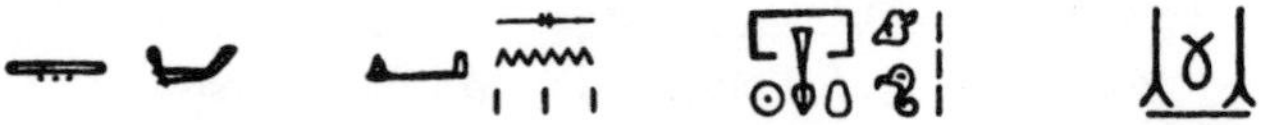

Ta-teser ṭā - sen per-χeru menχ

of Ta-tcheser, may they give sepulchral meals, linen garments,

sentrȧ merḥ χet nebt nefert ābt perert

incense, wax, thing every beautiful, pure, what appeareth

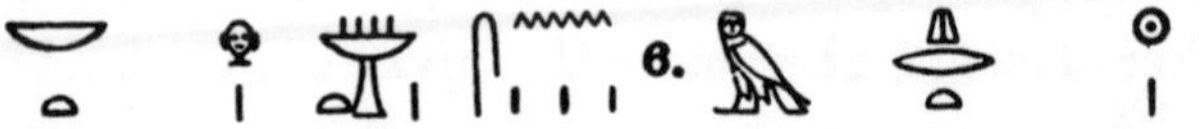

nebt ḥer χaut - sen em χert hru

{of every kind} upon altar their during the course of the day

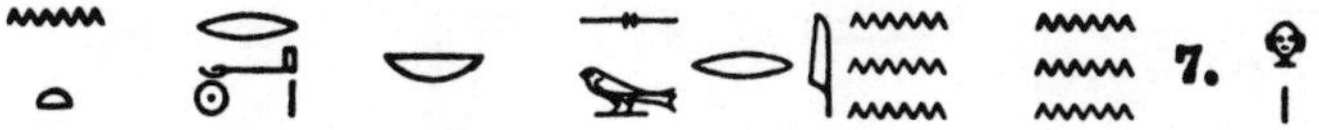

ent rā neb surà mu her

of day every, the drinking of water at

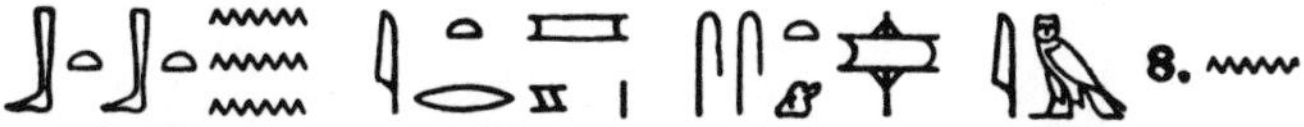

betbet àter seset àm en

the deepest part of the river, the breathing there of the

meht āq pert em Re-stau en

north wind, entrance and exit from Re-stau to the

ka en uā àqer hes en neter-f meru

double of the one perfect, favoured of his god, loving

neb - f her menχ - f ses

his lord by reason of his beneficence, following

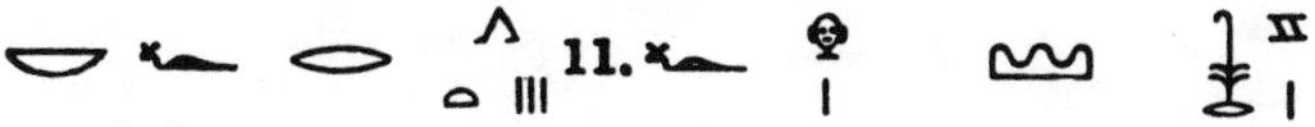

neb-f er utut - f her set rest

his lord on his expeditions over the country south

mehti suten sa mer χāu suten

[and] north, royal son, overseer of the weapons of the king,

Ȧnebni maā-χeru χer neteru paut

Anebni right of speech before the gods [and] the company

neteru

of the gods.

IV. Text from the CXXVth Chapter of the Book of the Dead.

[XVIIIth dynasty.]

2. 3.

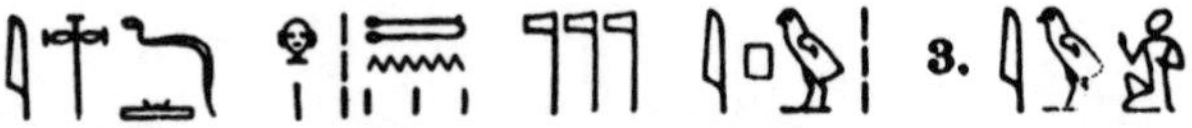

ȧneḳ ḥrȧu-θen neteru ȧpu ȧu-ȧ

Homage to you, O gods these! I,

reχ - kuȧ - ten reχ - kuȧ ren - ten enen

even I know you. I know your names. Do not

4.

χer - ȧ en šāt - ten enen

cast me down to your slaughtering knives, do not

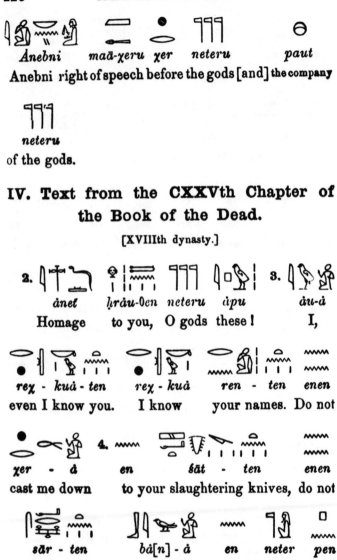

sār - ten bȧ[n] - ȧ en neter pen

bring forward ye my wickedness before god this

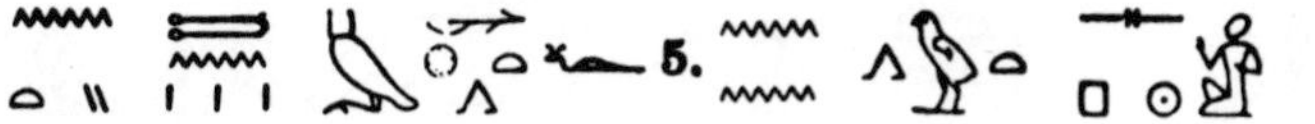

enti θen em χet - f enen iu-tu sep - à

whom ye follow him, let not come my moment

ḥer - ten tet̥ - ten maāt er - à embaḥ

before you. Declare ye right and truth for me before

ā Neb-er-t̥er ḥer entet àri - nà

the hand of Neb-er-tcher, because I have done

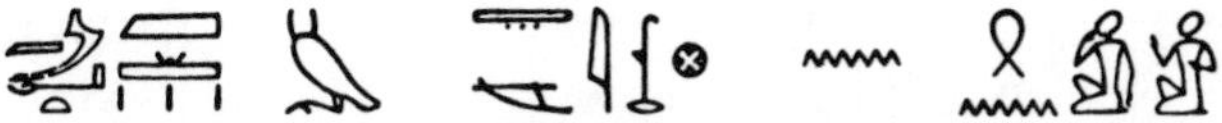

maāt em Ta-merà en šen - à

right and truth in Ta-mera [Egypt]. Not have I cursed

neter en iu sep - à ànet̥ ḥràu-ten

God, not hath come my moment. Homage to you,

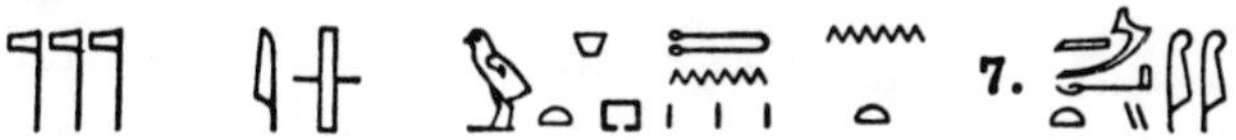

neteru àm useχt - θen ent maāti

O gods who live in your hall of right and truth,

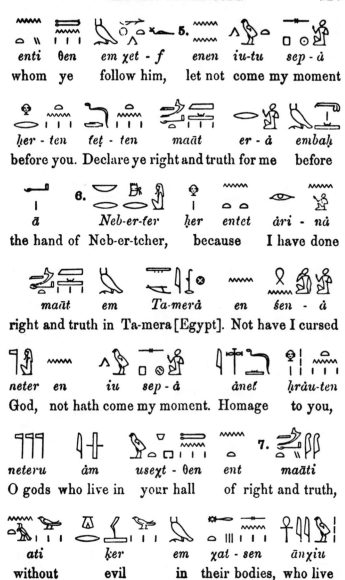

ati ḳer em χat - sen ānχiu

without evil in their bodies, who live

em maāt em Ȧnnu sāmiu
in right and truth in Annu, who consume

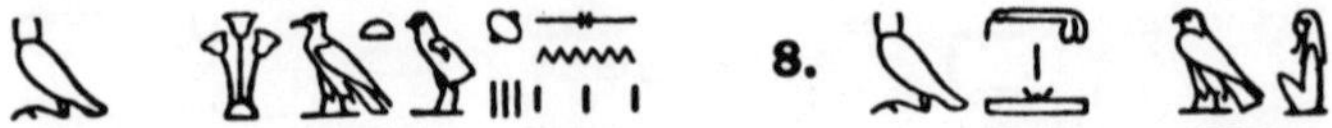

em ḥaut - sen 8. *em baḥ Ḥeru*
their entrails in the presence of Horus

ȧm ȧten - f neḥem - ten - uȧ mā
in his disk, deliver ye me from

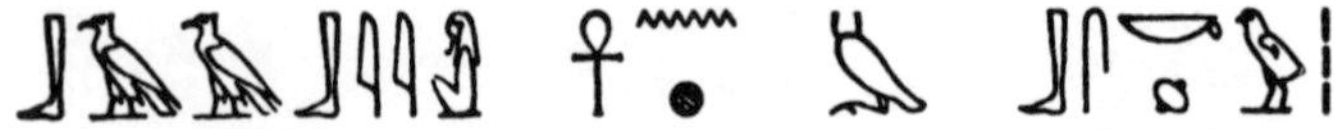

Baabi ānχ em beseku
Baabi, who liveth upon the intestines

seru hru pui en ȧpt āat
of the princes, on day that of the judgment great

mā - ten 9. *i - kuȧ χer - ten enen*
by you; I have come to you. Not

ȧsfet - ȧ enen χebent - ȧ en
have I committed faults, not have I sinned, not

ṭu - ȧ enen meteru - ȧ enen

have I done evil, not have I borne false witness, not

ȧri - nȧ χet eref ānχ - ȧ em

let be done to me anything therefore. I live in

10. 

maāt sām - ȧ em maāt

right and truth, I feed upon right and truth

ȧb - ȧ ȧu ȧri - nȧ ṭeṭet ret

my heart. I have done that which commanded men,

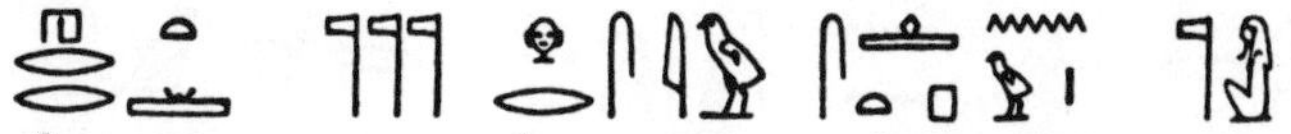

hereret neteru ḥer-s ȧu se-ḥetep-nuȧ neter

are satisfied the gods thereat. I have appeased God

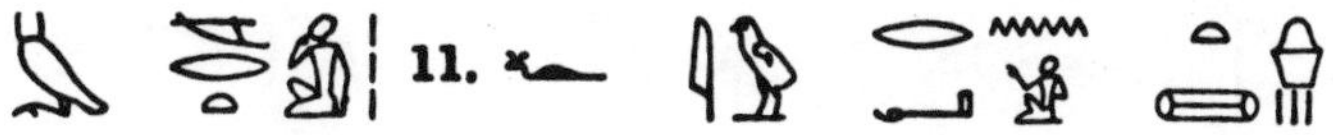

em mert - f ȧu erṭā - nȧ tau

by [doing] his will. I have given bread

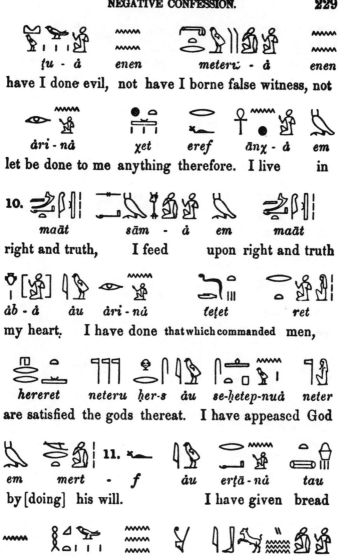

en ḥeqet mu en ȧbi

to the hungry, water to the thirsty,

ḥebs en ḥaiu māχen

clothes to the naked, and a boat

12.

dui ȧu ȧri - nȧ neter-ḥetepu en

to the shipwrecked. I have made offerings to the

neteru perχeru en χu neḥem-

gods, and sacrificial meals to the spirits. Deliver

ten - uȧ ȧr ten χu uȧ

ye me then ye, protect me

ȧr ten enen smȧ - ten er - ȧ em baḥ

then ye, not make accusation ye against me before

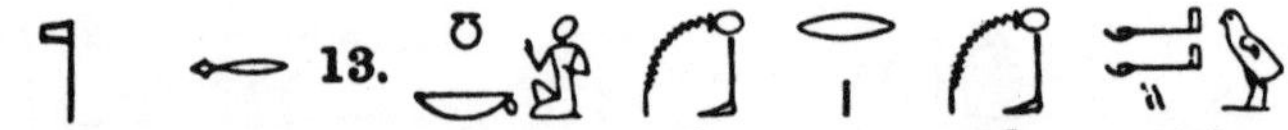

13.

neter āa nuk āb re āb āaiu

the god great. I am pure of mouth, pure of hands.

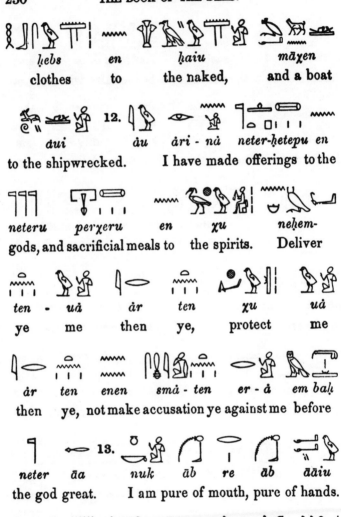

ṭeṭ - tu - nef iui sep sen ȧn maaiu

Is said to him, Come, twice, by those who see

su ḥer entet setem - nȧ meṭet tui
him, because I have heard speech that

teṭet en āa ḥenā mȧu em
spoken by the Donkey with the Cat in

per Ḥepṭ-re meteru - ȧ em
the house of Hept-re. I have borne testimony

ḥer - f ṭā - f tentu ȧu maa - nȧ
before him, he hath given the decision. I have seen

peseś ȧśeṭ em χennu
the division of the persea trees within

Re-stau nuk semiu - ȧ em baḥ
Re-stau. I, I offer up prayers in the presence of

neteru reχ χert χat - sen
the gods knowing what concerneth their persons.

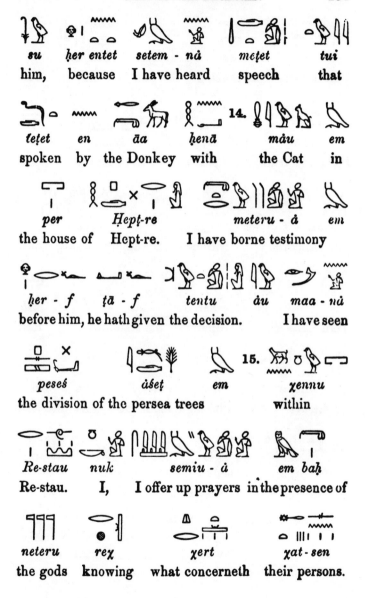

i - nȧ *āa* *er* *semeter*

I have come advancing to make a declaration of

16.

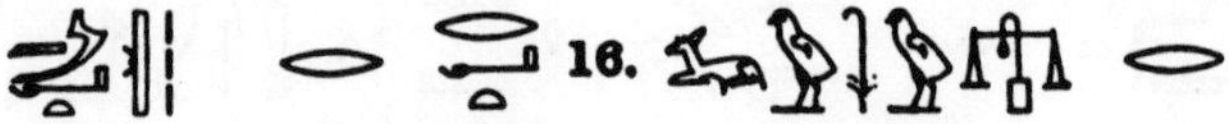

maāt *er* *erṭāt* *ȧusu* *er*

right and truth, to place the balance upon

āḥāu - f *em* *χennu* *ḳaȧu*

its supports within the amaranthine bushes.

ȧ *qa* *ḥer* *ȧat - f* *neb*

Hail exalted upon his standard, lord

atefu *ȧri* *ren - f* *em* *neb*

of the *atef* crown, making his name as the lord

17.

nifu *neḥem - kuȧ* *mā* *naik*

of winds, deliver me from thy

en *ȧputat* *uṭeṭiu*

messengers who make to happen

θemesu *seχeperiu* *àṭerit*

dire deeds, who make to arise calamities,

18.

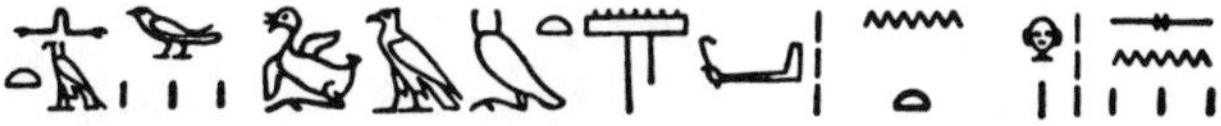

àt *tamet* *ent ḥràu-sen*

without covering upon their faces,

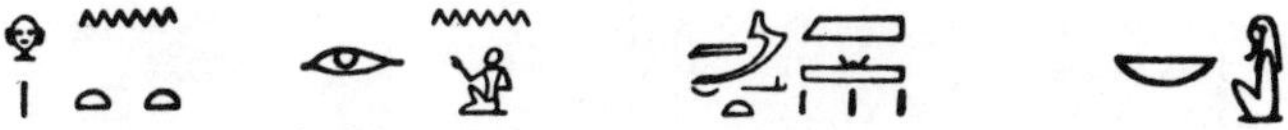

ḥer entet *àri - nà* *maāt* *neb*

because I have done right and truth. O lord of

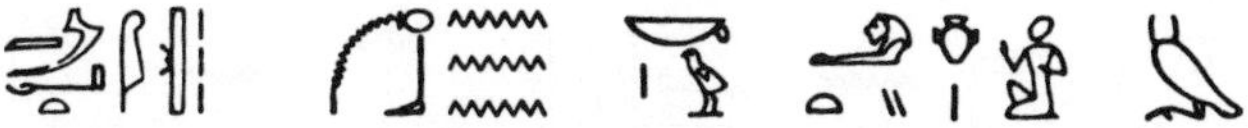

maāt *āb - kuà* *ḥāti - à* *em*

right and truth, I am pure, my breast is

19.

ābu *peḥi - à* *turà* *ḥer-àb-à*

washed, my hinder parts are cleansed, my interior

em *seśeṭit* *maāt* *enen*

[hath been] in the pool of right and truth, not [is]

āt *àm - à* *śu* *āb - nà* *em*

a member in me lacking. I have been purified in

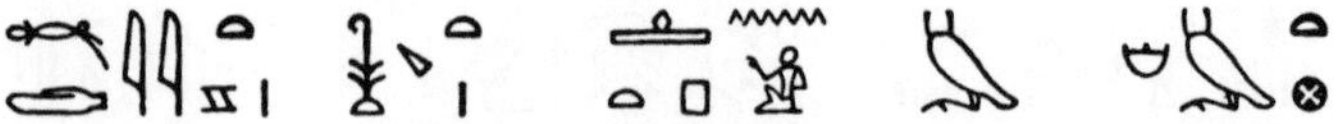

seśeṭit *reset* *ḥetep-nȧ* *em* *Ḥemt*

the pool southern, I have rested in Hemet,

20.

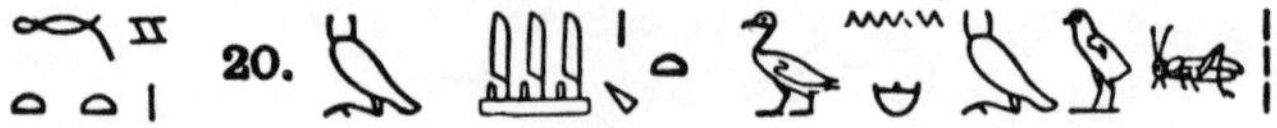

meḥtet *em* *seχet* *saneḥemu*

to the north of the field of the grasshoppers;

ābet *qeti* *ȧm - s* *em* *unnut*

bathe the divine sailors' in it at the season of

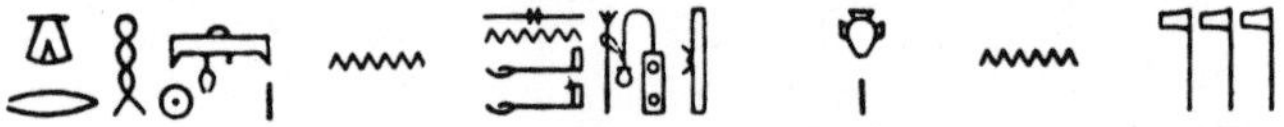

ḳerḥ *en* *senāā* *ȧb* *en* *neteru*

night to gratify (?) the heart of the gods

21.

em *χet* *seś-ȧ* *ḥer-s* *em* *ḳerḥ*

after I have passed over it by night and

em *hru* *ṭāu* *iut - f* *ȧn - sen* *er - ȧ*

by day. They grant his coming, they say to me,

nimā *trȧ* *tu* *ȧn - sen* *er - ȧ*

Who then art thou? say they to me.

pu trȧ ren - k ȧn - sen er - ȧ

What then is thy name? say they to me.

22.

nuk ruṭ χeri en ḥait ȧmi

I grow among the flowers dwelling in

baaq ren - ȧ seś-nek ḥer mā

the olive tree is my name. Pass on thou forthwith,

ȧn - sen er - ȧ seś-nȧ ḥer nut

say they unto me. I have passed by the town

meḥtet baat peti trȧ maa - nek

north of the bushes. What then didst thou see

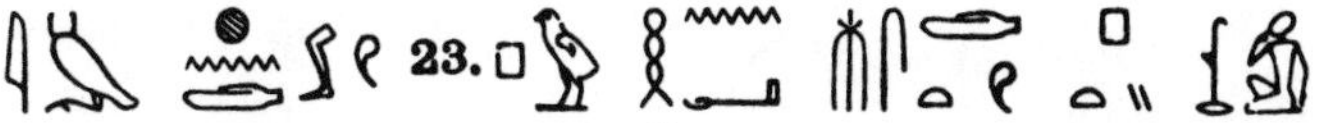

23.

ȧm χenṭ pu ḥenā mesṭet peti trȧ

there? The leg and the thigh. What then

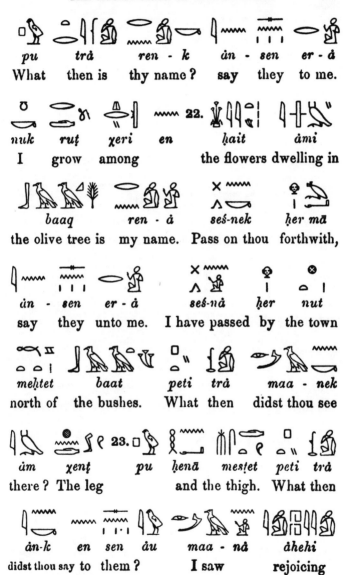

ȧn-k en sen ȧu maa - nȧ ȧhehi

didst thou say to them? I saw rejoicing

em ennu taiu Fenχu peti trȧ

in those lands of the Fenkhu. What then

24.

erṭāt-sen nek besu pu en seśet

did give they to thee? A flame it was of fire,

ḥenā uaṫ en θeḥent peti trȧ

together with a tablet of crystal. What then

ȧri - nek eres ȧu qeres - nȧ set ḥer

didst thou do therewith? I buried them by

uteb en maāti em χet χaui

the furrow of Maāti with the things of the night.

25.

peti trȧ qem - nek ȧm ḥer uteb

What then didst thou find there by the furrow

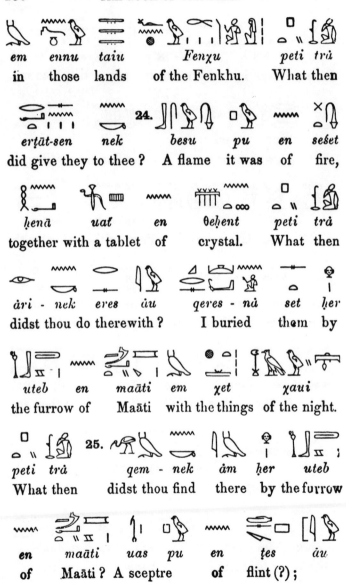

en maāti uas pu en ṭes ȧu

of Maāti? A sceptre of flint (?);

seśeṭ - nek su petrȧ ȧref

maketh to prevail thee it. What then is [the name of]

su uas pu en ṭes erṭā nifu

the sceptre of flint? Giver of winds

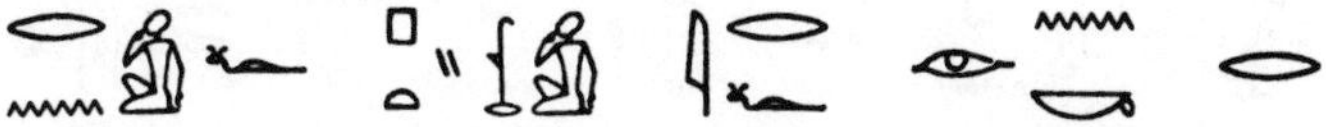

ren - f peti trȧ ȧref ȧri - nek er

is its name. What then therefore didst thou do with

pa besu en seśet ḥenā pa

the flame of fire and with the

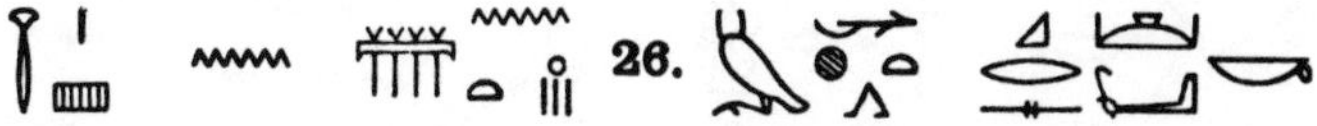

26.

uaṭ en θeḥent em χet qeres-k

tablet of crystal after thou didst bury

set ȧu hatu-nȧ ḥer-s ȧu

them? I uttered words over it,

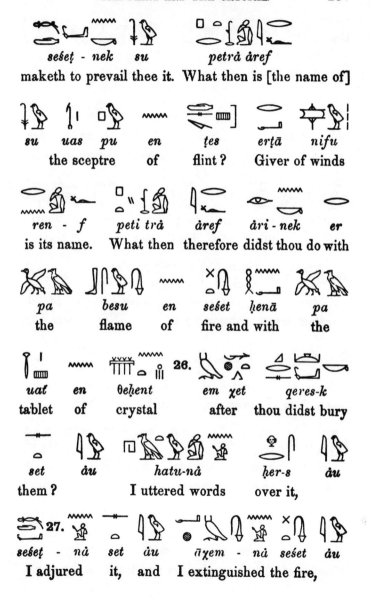

27.

seśeṭ - nȧ set ȧu āχem - nȧ seśet ȧu

I adjured it, and I extinguished the fire,

28.

seṭ - nȧ uat em qemam

I made use of the tablet in creating

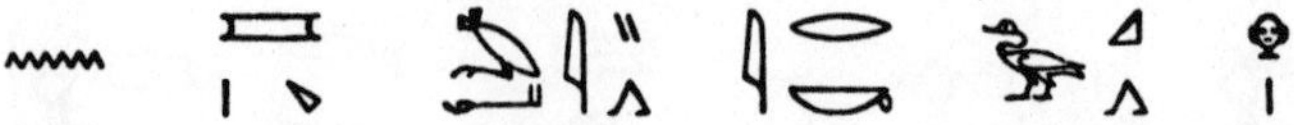

en mer māȧi ȧrek āq ḥer

a pool of water. Come then pass in over

sba pen en useχt ten ent Maāti

door this of Hall this of Maāti,

29.

ȧu - k reχ - θȧ - n enen(i.e., ȧn) ṭā - ȧ

thou art knowing us. Not will I let

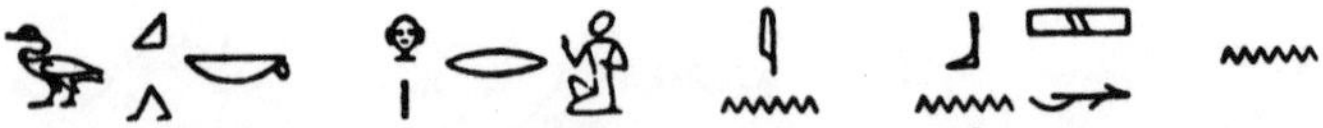

āq - k ḥer - ȧ ȧn benś en

enter thee over me, saith the bolt of

30.

sba pen [ȧ]n-ȧs teṭ - nek ren - ȧ

door this, except thou sayest my name.

teχ en bu maā ren - t

Weight of the place of right and truth is thy name.

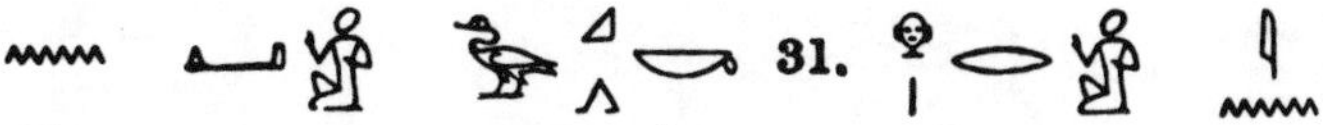

ȧn *ṭā - ȧ* *āq - k* 31. *ḥer - ȧ* *ȧn*

Not will let I enter thee by me, saith

ārit *unem* *ent* *sba* *pen*

the post right of door this,

[*ȧ*]*n - ȧs* *ṭeṭ - nek* *ren - ȧ* 32. *ḥenku - nef*

except thou sayest my name. He weigheth

fat *maāt* *ren-t* *enen*(*i.e.*, *ȧn*)

the labours of right and truth is thy name. Not

ṭā - ȧ *āq - k* *ḥer-ȧ* 33. *ȧn* *ārit*

will I let enter thee by me, saith the post

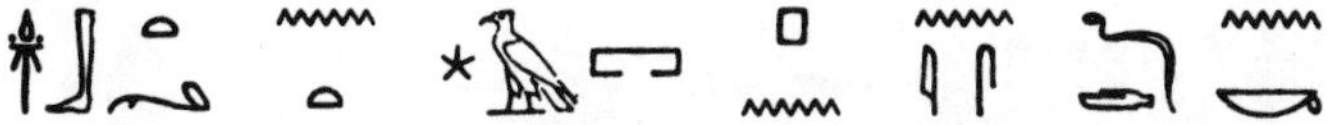

ȧbet *ent* *sba* *pen* [*ȧ*]*n-ȧs* *ṭeṭ - nek*

left of door this, except thou sayest

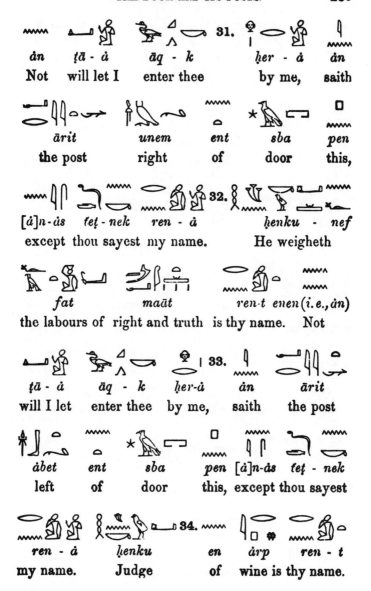

ren - ȧ *ḥenku* 34. *en* *ȧrp* *ren - t*

my name. Judge of wine is thy name.

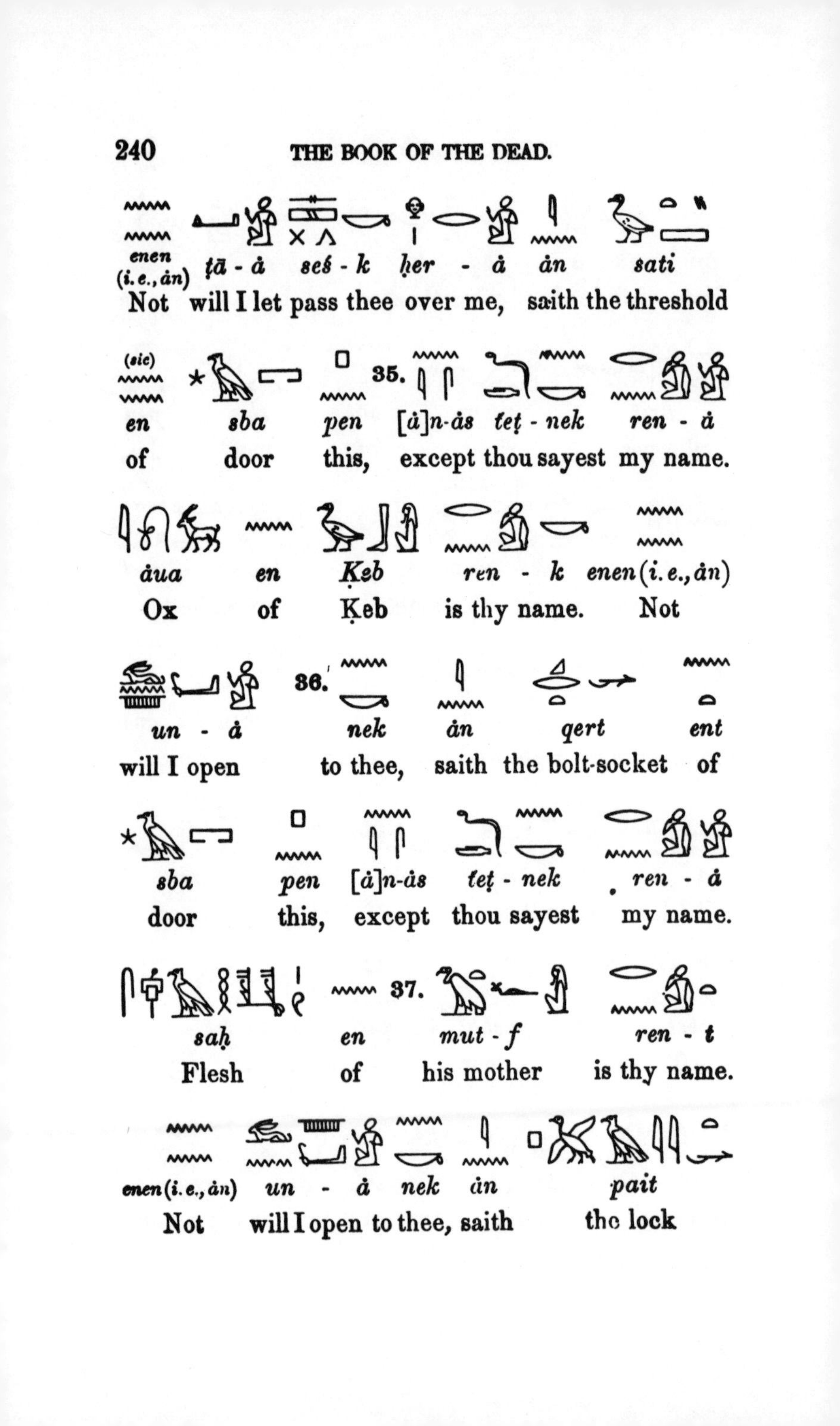

enen (*i.e., ån*) *ṭā - å seś - k ḥer - å ån sati*
Not will I let pass thee over me, saith the threshold

(*sic*) *en sba pen* 35. [*å*]*n-ås ṭeṭ - nek ren - å*
of door this, except thou sayest my name.

åua en Ḳeb ren - k enen (*i.e., ån*)
Ox of Ḳeb is thy name. Not

un - å 36. *nek ån qert ent*
will I open to thee, saith the bolt-socket of

sba pen [*å*]*n-ås ṭeṭ - nek ren - å*
door this, except thou sayest my name.

saḥ en 37. *mut - f ren - t*
Flesh of his mother is thy name.

enen (*i.e., ån*) *un - å nek ån pait*
Not will I open to thee, saith the lock

en sba pen [å]n ås tet - nek ren - å

of door this, except thou sayest my name.

ānχet utat ent Sebek neb

Liveth the *utchat* of Sebek, the lord of

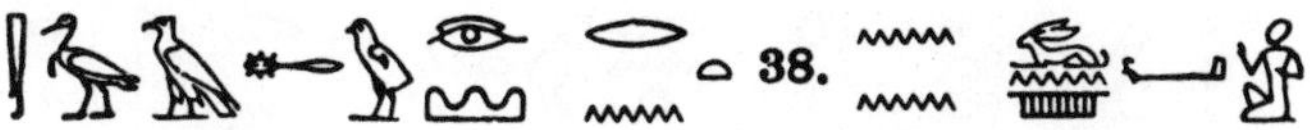

Baχau ren-t 38. *enen (ån) un - å*

Bakhau, is thy name. Not will I open

nek enen (ån) tā - å āq - k her - å ån

to thee, not will I let pass thee over me, saith

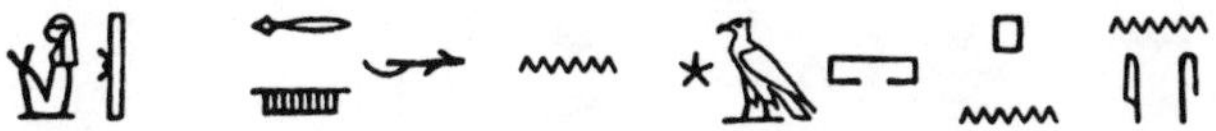

åri āa en sba pen [å]n ås

the dweller at the door of door this, except

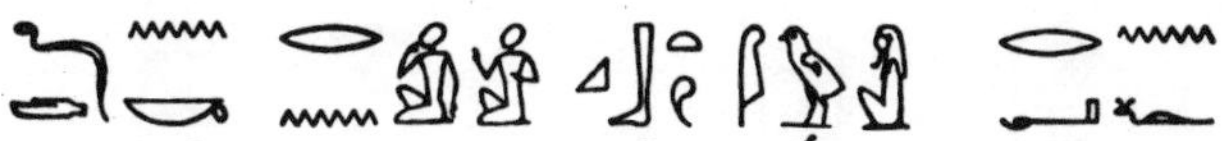

tet - nek ren - å qebt Śu ertā-nef

thou tellest my name. Arm of Shu that placeth itself

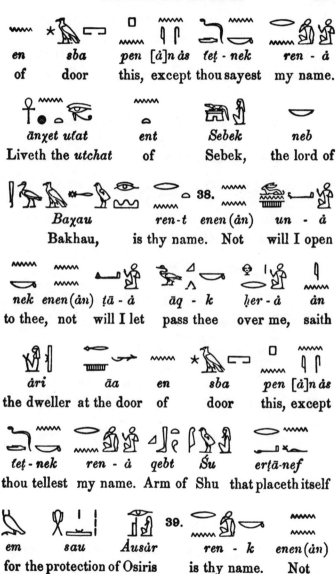

em sau Ausår 39. *ren - k enen (ån)*

for the protection of Osiris is thy name. Not

ṭā - n seś - k ḥer - n ȧn ḥeptu

will we allow to pass thee by us, say the posts

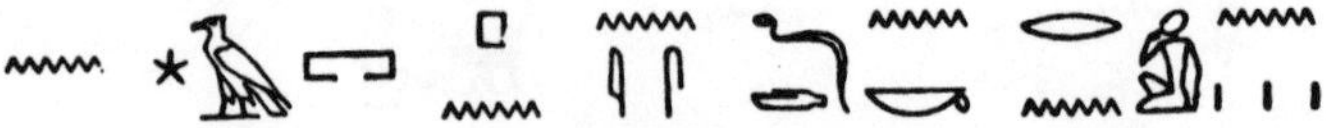

en sba pen [ȧn] ȧs teṭ - nek ren - n

of door this, except thou sayest our names.

neχenu nu Rennut ren-ten

Serpent children of Rennut are your names.

40.

ȧu - k reχ - θȧ - n seś ȧrek ḥer - n

Thou knowest us, pass then by us.

enen (ȧn) χenṭ - k ḥer - ȧ ȧn sati

Not shalt tread thou upon me, saith the floor

en useχt ten [ȧn] ȧs teṭ - k

of hall this, except thou sayest

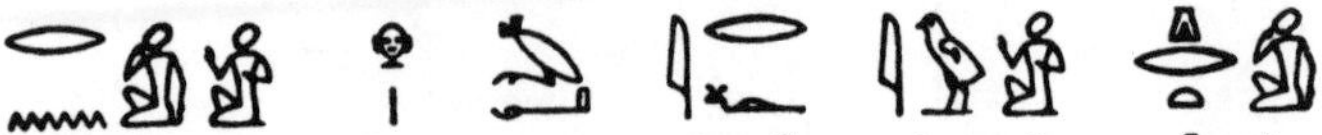

ren - ȧ ḥer mā ȧref ȧu - ȧ ḳert

my name. . . . . I am silent,

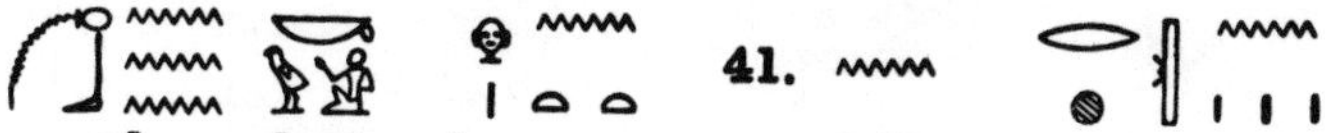

āb - kuȧ ḥer entet 41. *[ȧ]n reχ - n*

I am pure, because not do we know

reṭ - k χenṭ - k ḥer - n ȧm - sen

thy two legs thou treadest upon us with them;

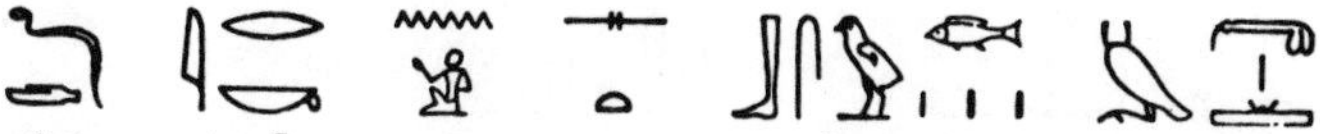

ṭeṭ ȧrek nȧ set besu em baḥ

tell then to me them. Traveller before

Ȧmsu ren en reṭ - ȧ unemi

Menu (or, Amsu) is the name of my leg right.

unpet ent Nebt-ḥet ren en 42. *reṭ - ȧ*

Grief of Nephthys is the name of my leg

ȧbi χenṭ ȧrek ḥer - n ȧu - k

left. Tread then upon us, thou

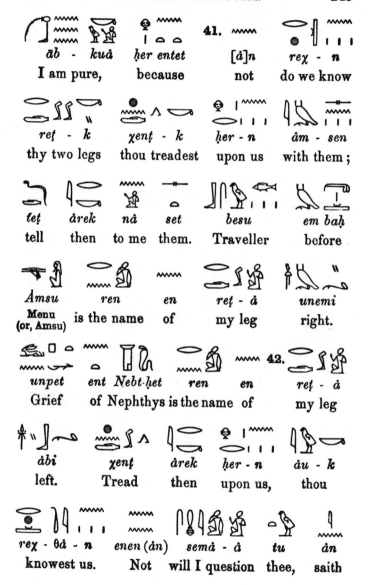

reχ - θȧ - n enen (ȧn) semȧ - ȧ tu ȧn

knowest us. Not will I question thee, saith

åri āa en useχt θen [å]n ås
the guardian of the door of hall this, except

43.
teṭ - nek ren - å sa åbu ťār
thou sayest my name. Discerner of hearts, searcher of

χat ren - k semå - å tu åref
reins, is thy name. I will question thee then.

nimā en neter åmi unnut - f
Who is the god dwelling in his hour?

teṭ - k set en māau taui
Speak thou it. The recorder of the two lands.

44.
peti trå ṣu māau taui
Who then is he the recorder of the two lands?

Teḥuti pu māå ån Teḥuti i - nek
Thoth it is. Come, saith Thoth, come thou

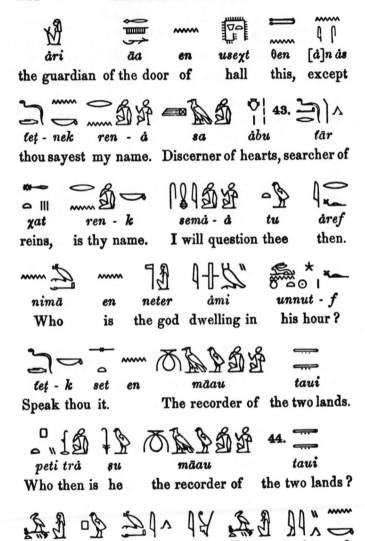

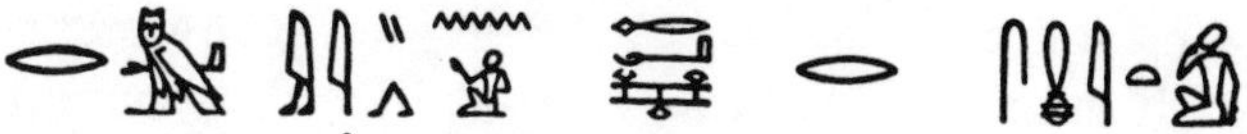

er mā i - nȧ āā er semȧt

hither (?). I come advancing to the examination.

peti trȧ χert - k ȧu-ȧ āb - kuȧ

What then is thy condition? I, I am pure

45. *em χu neb ȧu χu - nuȧ*

from evil all. I am protected

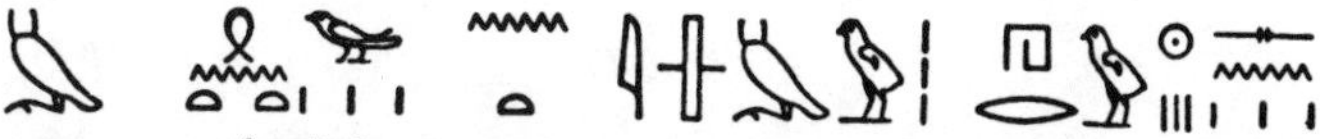

em šentet ent ȧmu hru - sen

from the baleful acts of those who live in their days,

enen (ȧn) tuȧ emmā - sen semȧ - ȧ ȧref

not am I among them. I have examined then

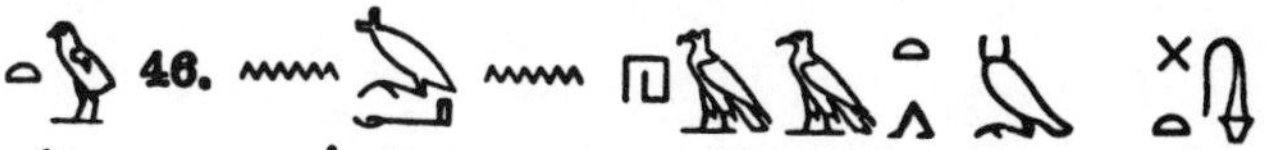

46. *tu nimā en haat em sešet*

thee. Who goeth down into the flame,

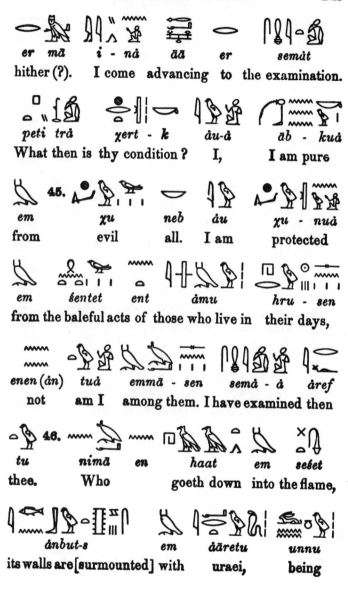

ȧnbut-s em ȧāretu unnu

its walls are [surmounted] with uraei, being

satu - f *em* *ennu* *ui*

his paths in that same lake?

sebi *pu* 47. *Ȧsȧr* *pu* *uṭa* *ȧrek*

The traverser Osiris is. Come forward then,

māketu *smȧ - θȧ* *ȧu* *tau - k*

verily thou hast been examined; is thy bread

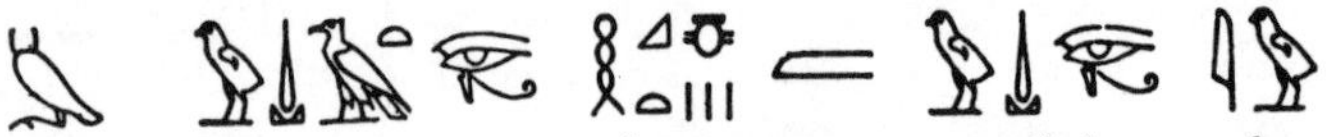

em *uṭat* *ḥeqt* *em* *uṭat* *ȧu*

from the *utchat,* and [thy] beer from the *utchat,* are

per - tu *nek* *χeru* *ṭep* *ta*

brought out to thee sepulchral offerings upon earth

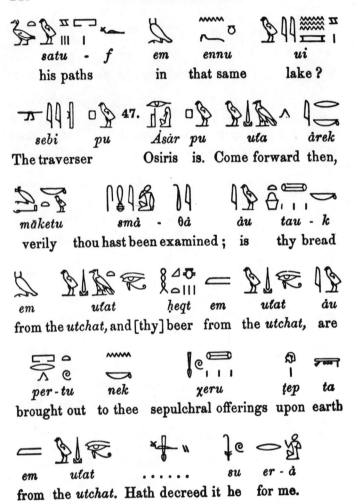

em *uṭat* . . . . . . *su* *er - ȧ*

from the *utchat.* Hath decreed it he for me.